The Smoked Seafood Cookbook

The Smoked Seafood Cookbook

Easy, Innovative Recipes from America's Best Fish Smokery

T.R. Durham

Proprietor, Durham's Tracklements and Smokery, Ann Arbor

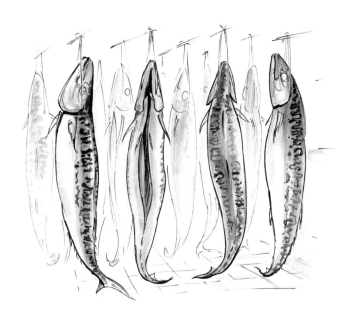

The University of Michigan Press   Ann Arbor

Copyright © by the University of Michigan 2008
All rights reserved
Published in the United States of America by
The University of Michigan Press
Manufactured in China
⊗ Printed on acid-free paper

2011 2010 2009 2008 4 3 2 1

A CIP catalog record for this book is available from the British Library.

Library of Congress Cataloging-in-Publication Data

Durham, T. R., 1942–
       The smoked seafood cookbook : easy, innovative recipes from
    America's best fish smokery / T.R. Durham.
          p.   cm.
       Includes bibliographical references and index.
       ISBN-13: 978-0-472-11674-4 (cloth : alk. paper)
       ISBN-10: 0-472-11674-6 (cloth : alk. paper)
       1. Cookery (Smoked foods) 2. Cookery (Seafood) 3. Smoked fish.
    I. Title.
    TX835.D87   2008
    641.6'92—dc22   2008017959

Text design and typesetting by Joseph Mooney

For Susan, who despite long-standing, overwhelming evidence to the contrary, has had the audacity to insist that I could actually put something in writing.

Acknowledgments

If any book is clearly the outcome of a sustained joint effort, this is it. In this case by Joe Mooney, my editor at the University of Michigan Press, and by my wife Susan Douglas. Joe provided the initiative, in concept and enthusiasm, for the project, along with a considerable amount of his own time to keep things moving and organized—not to mention great patience and tact. Susan provided many recipes tweaked and re-tweaked, sustenance on all fronts, and not a few strategically timed and placed swift kicks of the sort required repeatedly to move the proverbial Missouri mule.

Of course, without the Tracklements and Smokery, there would be no hook to hang this on. Much gratitude is due to all those whose support, by their enthusiasm for our products or by working alongside me at the smokery, has made so oxymoronic an enterprise (smoking ocean fish in the upper Midwest) not only possible but deeply enjoyable. Many thanks to Tracklements' customers in Ann Arbor, too. They have made the retail part of the smokery a source of constant rejuvenation through their loyalty and their ongoing conversation on food and restaurants, travel, crime (fiction), politics, economy, children's education, and more food.

Some in particular stand out for their very early discovery of Tracklements and great support of the shop in Kerrytown and continuing discussions on many fronts: Ricky and Bernie, Ken and Anne, Ray, Kay, Terry, Steve, Arthur, Charles and Julia, Aileen, Julie and Bob, Charlotte, another Steve, Dan, Kathleen, Ken and Wendy, Eve, Gauri, Brendan, Marylen, Ernest, Rhea and Leslie, Sandy, Carol and Mary, Ben, Alan, Julie, Carroll and Alvia, Fernando and Julie, Sonya and Guenter, Gabrielle and Paul, Kate and Ed, Phil and Mary, Kathleen and Hubert, Smilka and Dan . . .

At the smokery, Margarito Dominguez has been doing much of the heavy lifting throughout the year and for peak holiday production for the past four years. His good cheer and meticulous attention to every aspect of our operation have been indispensable. Our retail and mail order services have been greatly enhanced over the years by Ellen, Ryan, Samu, and more recently Alycia, Joanna,

Kara, Jacob, and Tricia. Each has brought a distinctive personal style, a fondness for our customers, special talents, valued companionship.

Perhaps it's worth mentioning my brother Jim, who wisely steered me away from barbecue and toward salmon, and provided the seed money necessary to become more like a business and less like a backyard hobby (although he stimulated that as well).

Contents

Introduction

I run a smokehouse in Ann Arbor—Durham's Tracklements and Smokery—that specializes in smoked fish. The three questions I get the most are "How long have you been here?" (ten years and counting), "What else can I do with this besides put it on a bagel?" and "Is farmed salmon really bad for you?" Responses to the second question have included suggestions written on scraps of paper towels, exchanges with customers in which we trade ideas (Ann Arbor is, after all, known for its rather intense and accomplished "foodie" population), and more formal serving suggestions offered in our literature. Responses to the third question involve, often, a somewhat intemperate rant best labeled "The bogus war against farmed salmon." My shop is small; many of my customers know me well (and vice versa), so they put up with this. Some even enjoy it. But because there is, in fact, quite a bit you can do with smoked fish beyond blanketing a bagel with it, and because many of the folks who come into the shop want to know more about smoked fish—including whether farmed salmon is evil—I thought I'd put these recipes and rants on paper.

Some Tracklements customers have expressed horror at the thought of cooking with our smoked fish, saying simply, "It's too good to *cook* with!" But their numbers have been offset by those who have tried one or another of our serving suggestions and then sent us their own special variation on the basic recipe.

Then there's the horror at using a luxurious delicacy like smoked seafood in any way other than the classically simple slice, perhaps with bread or crackers and a light dusting of freshly ground black pepper. Fortunately, the end pieces and tail cuts from Tracklements provide a product that holds up well in an array of culinary uses and is quite affordable, too. A little goes a long way—and makes a big difference.

We tend to think of smoked-salmon or smoked-seafood appetizers as uncooked, room-temperature concoctions, assembled with fresh or ready-made ingredients. And as we will see, there's quite a fetching variety of such preparations. But the judicious application of heat can, with the proper mixture of ingredients and deftness of hand, result in a truly extraordinary delicacy.

This is a totally different cookbook, then. I am a recovering academic, having spent twenty-five years presenting ideas to the eager young minds of America before deciding that rubbing dry-salt cure on fish might be better suited to my temperament, and possibly more productive. But old habits die hard, and in the process of running the shop I have learned a great deal about smoked fish and history, smoked fish and politics, and smoked fish and culture that many people don't know but find interesting. So this cookbook has two parts: short essays about the history of and controversies surrounding smoked fish and, of course, the recipes.

I started this business in Amherst, Massachusetts, when my brother—what was he thinking?—sent me a Hondo smoker the size and shape of a small locomotive that arrived on the back of a Yellow Freight 18-wheeler. (It now attractively graces our backyard, where my wife tries to convince the neighbors that it's what she calls "a sculpting.") Within the orbit of New York, Boston, and Philadelphia, the dominant smoked fish was salmon, Scottish or Irish or lox, and, to a lesser extent, sable and bluefish. When I moved the business to Ann Arbor, I was in the region of smoked whitefish and chubs. And then there had been those trips to Britain, which is where it all started.

In the pubs along the back roads of Scotland, Yorkshire, Cornwall, and Devon, the "locally oak-smoked" trout and especially mackerel were essential accompaniments to the pint. Here, kippers—grilled herring—for breakfast were a surprisingly welcome offering of many B&Bs. In Scotland I had the great honor to meet Duncan Stewart—Dunky to all who knew him—the caretaker of the flat we were renting. Dunky often started the day with a few wee drams of Scotch, meaning that by midday, when he was smoking mackerel and salmon for half the people in the village, he welcomed some assistance, and I was pressed into duty. It was in Scotland and England that I learned how to smoke fish and got a glimpse of the role smoked fish could play in everyday cooking. Yes, something praiseworthy about British food.

As a result of travel, reading, moving around, and getting tips and requests from the shop's well-traveled and food-serious clientele, Tracklements now offers various cures of cold- and warm-smoked salmon, smoked trout, sable, bluefish, haddock, and scallops. These fish can do much more than grace a cracker. Smoked fish can transform soups and stews, invigorate pasta, redefine sushi, liven up casseroles, grace salads, and serve as garnishes on all kinds of dishes. So this cookbook will include a range of cuisines from around the world and various kinds of dishes.

Smoked fish has a history, it is embedded in politics, it has a variety of traits and uses depending on the fish, and it is discussed, debated, and often misrepresented in the press. It is this history, lore, folklore, and fact that I also want to present to readers interested in the interplay between food and culture. For those who just want to cook, you can jump ahead to the recipes. For those who want the background, I hope this introduction will provide some armchair food tourism and help sort out food fiction from fact.

Smoked Fish and Your Diet

No, this is not a smoked-fish diet cookbook; even my wife couldn't afford that, and I give her a pretty good deal on things. But by now most people know that salmon and other more oily fish are rich in omega-3 fatty acids that are very good for you and may reduce your risk of heart disease and promote the production of "good" (HDL) cholesterol and reduce the production of "bad" (LDL) cholesterol. Some studies have even found that omega-3 fatty acids are a benefit to children's learning and development, and many of my customers have been somewhat dismayed at how much their kids like smoked salmon, hoovering it up off the plate before the parents get their fair share. Because smoked fish is a high-protein, low-calorie, yet delicious food, it works very well both with low-carb diets and with those that emphasize a mix of proteins, veg, and grains. Using smoked fish as part of whatever diet you may be on is good for you and makes you feel less deprived because it also feels like a great indulgence.

Channeling Elizabeth David

We should all channel the great food writer Elizabeth David. David grew up in England during the early twentieth century. English food back then had a pretty bad reputation—there wasn't anything the British wouldn't boil into tasteless, sodden submission. As luck would have it, David went to the Sorbonne and, later, worked for the Ministry of Information during World War II and lived in France, Italy, Greece, and Egypt, where she discovered real food. After the war, when she returned to London, David began writing food articles at a time when English "cuisine" may have been at its nadir. She published *A Book of Mediterranean Food,* followed by *French Country Cooking, Summer Cooking,* and *Italian Food.* These were not mere recipe books, and they did not go in for the forty-two step preparations of three-star French restaurants. Instead, David often offered brief descriptions of the recipes intermixed with accounts of where they came from and how they evolved, thus conveying to the reader a spirit of informality and improvisation.

Smoked seafood fits easily into the approach often taken by David in her cookbooks, especially *Summer Cooking*—simple, informal, improvisational. David often provided several variations on a dish, each version encouraging the reader to conjure others. Often the "cooking" or the "recipe" was more like freestyle shopping for a picnic, or simply putting one together from what happened to be in the fridge and pantry. The principle was the serendipitous discovery of several ingredients that just go together. This approach is especially suited to the rapidly expanding and evolving array of foodstuffs from around the world and to the increasing variety of locally produced, seasonal specialties. It is also very well suited to the emerging concern about food's "carbon footprint"—how much energy is consumed producing and shipping foodstuffs around the world. If you're channeling David, the local farmers' market is one of the best places to find ingredients to mix and match. A somewhat similar approach guides Michael Field's *Culinary Classics and Improvisations*—really, many things you can do with leftovers! In our case, smoked fish and seafood are the culinary classics, with many variations on accompaniments left to the inspirations of experience and what's ready to hand.

Tracklements Defined

What are tracklements, anyway? Coined by Dorothy Hartley, a British folklorist and food writer, in her 1950s book *Food in England,* the word *tracklements* refers to relishes, mustards, chutneys, or jellies served to accompany meat dishes such as the iconic British "roast joint" or leg of lamb. Hartley claims to have taken liberties with the spelling of the somewhat archaic term *trucklements* from Scotland and the Borders, meaning bits and pieces of personal baggage one carries around—or, less felicitously, "impedimenta." Clearly, some liberties have been taken to expand the meaning to accompaniments, as for a dinner, festive occasion or celebration, or more casual get-together. As the recipes here suggest, many of our tracklements can be easily carried around, either on communal serving platters or as individual bite-sized treats, thus preserving some of the term's early etymology.

This cookbook is an attempt to link the making to the using and enjoying, in many instances drawing on suggestions and ideas from the folks who have accompanied their occasions with something from Tracklements and generously provided the feedback that makes anticipating customers' enjoyment of our products that much more possible.

Here you will find recipes inspired by cooks, family, friends, and customers, and several from well-known food-world pros. While plenty feature smoked salmon, other smoked fish—cod, haddock, trout, mackerel, sable, scallops, catfish, hake, bluefish—receive due attention. The emphasis is on easily assembled, easily presented, and easily consumed—no need for a food stylist! You'll also find new combinations of flavors and textures and recipes with suggestions for further improvisation. And, happily, many of the smoked-seafood ingredients have become more widely available in recent years.

The Assembly Principle

We all know the two, and only two, conventions about serving smoked salmon or other smoked seafood. One, put it on a bagel. Or, alternately, have it star as a centerpiece of the appetizer, hors d'oeuvre, or canapé table, especially in bite-sized compositions that may emphasize appearance and elegance over effect on the palate. End of story. Maybe this very narrow repertoire is due to smoked salmon's connotations of luxury and expense, or to the simple elegance of its appearance. Whatever the origin and results of these conventions, the truth is that smoked salmon, whether cold- or hot-smoked, is welcome in a wide range of presentations. Its color, texture, and richness serve ably alongside an assortment of greens, herbs, breads, crackers, spreads, and condiments. With the availability of ingredients from Asia, South America, the Middle East, and Mediterranean areas, and the explosion in international cooking, it is time to free smoked salmon from its bagel and canapé straitjacket. Plus, there are other luscious smoked fishes that are terrific and underappreciated additions to a host of dishes.

The assembly principle rests on the simple practice of combining several high-quality ingredients in delicious, healthful, and easy-to-do combinations. Think BLT without, of course, the bacon (or having to cook it). The assembly principle has these clear advantages. It's quick. It's elegant. You can tailor it to your tastes: you assemble the ingredients you like and eliminate the ones you don't. It's healthy (although there is room for occasional indulgences). And it encourages home cooks to be creative and allows them to improvise and be flexible. But most of all, it's easy, especially if you only have a half hour to get a meal on the table.

Back to the two classic ways of serving smoked salmon that many are familiar with, even if they've never actually had direct contact with either. One of course is the bagel and lox of New York delicatessen fame. The other is smoked salmon on bread or cracker of choice with capers, chopped onion, hard-boiled egg, black pepper, and maybe a squirt of lemon. The salmon may be affixed to the bread or cracker with unsalted butter, cream cheese, or crème fraîche, or perhaps one of the latter two mixed with sour cream.

So far, so good—except, perhaps, which bread, which cracker, why the capers and onion, and what else might substitute for any and all, except the salmon? Over the years at the smokery, customer inquiries, suggestions, and feedback on our own "self-catering" smoked-salmon platters have led to a number of alternatives to this basic template. Some of these utilize familiar ingredients not customarily substituted for the standards. And some use ingredients only recently familiar, due to new cuisines, new growers and purveyors, new restaurants, and new chefs.

Not that some of the standard ingredients don't invite substitutions. Capers, for example: they can be quite salty, mushy rather than crisp, gray rather than greenish, and they have a habit of rolling off onto the floor. Onion, red or otherwise, can be harsh and bitter, rather than sweetly biting, and is often simply overpowering. Better on a burger. Crackers themselves vary in size, flakiness, seasoning, and saltiness, and have a tendency to fracture unpredictably onto clothing, furniture, and carpeting. The entire model eschews green-crisp-fresh as an essential component.

The recipes in this book illustrate some of the variations reliably available at supermarkets and farmers' markets, perhaps with a side trip to a specialty or Asian food store. They are meant to be tried as is but even more to suggest new, exploratory directions to follow on one's own. With the assembly principle, you can play with distinct ingredients, and you might not need to rely as much on kitchen appliances such as blenders or food processors. Many of these recipes take a slice or dice approach, illustrated by the Chunky Smoked-Trout Spread in the first chapter, as compared with a puree, blend together, mousse-spread mode. While some of these recipes are long-standing personal favorites, the slice-dice-mix-dress style stresses the complementarity of individual ingredients. This is not only tasty in itself but, I think, is more inviting of experiments in alternative compositions, making it possible to separate out more clearly the part played by one ingredient and hence to think about just what else might fit in nicely.

Cooking with Smoked Fish and Seafood

Here smoked fish and seafood are used as ingredients in cooked dishes—brandades, fritters, gratins, chowders—where they mingle with potato, pasta, rice, and greens and their flavors suffuse rather than punctuate a dish. Because of this, and because warmer dishes tend to accentuate the salty taste for a given level of salt, these dishes require more attentiveness to both the salt and smoke of the seafood ingredients. Balancing these characteristics to achieve the desired final state, with the seafood blending nicely with other ingredients, is not made easier by the wide variations encountered in different smoked fish from different styles or sources. Most published recipes ignore this issue, stating simply a quantity of a type of smoked fish or seafood to be used (too often even failing to specify cold- or hot-smoked versions). This matter is addressed, but only partially, in the "Sources" section. In the end, you'll want to be taste-familiar with the particular smoked ingredient you plan to use. If possible, sample taste at the point of purchase. If you're fortunate enough to have a purveyor who has tasted products from various sources, and especially one who has done some of this kind of cooking, ask for advice. But as a last-ditch precaution, don't add salt beyond what is in the fish at the cooking stage—wait until serve and taste time!

Smoked Seafood: Lure and Lore

It takes more than smoke to make smoked seafood—or smoked anything else for that matter. The pre-smoking process is just as important as the smoking itself. Of course, the quality of what you start with is crucial to the final result, but those qualities can be enhanced, complemented, or subdued—even subjugated—in the process to follow.

Curing comes first—this makes the fish smokable, able to hold up for lengthy time periods to smoking at slightly below or above room temperature. Curing can be done "dry," with a mixture of salt, perhaps some sugar, and seasonings applied directly to the flesh. Or it can be done "wet" or brined, with the curing ingredients dissolved in water. And it can be done fast or slow. In general, previously frozen and thawed fish must be brined or wet-cured. Larger fillets of fresh fish can be dry-cured. Smaller fillets and whole fish are most easily brined. More on this in the section on do-it-yourself smoking.

Most of us over the past few years have learned that brining adds flavor and preserves moisture before cooking. Much the same can be done in curing fish for smoking. As with smoke, adding flavor can be a fine thing to do. Often, however, these additions can overwhelm the character of the particular kind of fish to be smoked. Some of the spices and herbs or other seasoning ingredients offer more than simple flavorings to the final product. They can work with the particular kind of fish to better develop and present the special character of the fish itself. There are places that can turn out smoked salmon, halibut, trout, sable, even scallops and other seafood varieties, and the only way you can tell the difference is by reading the label—and even with that prompting it may be nearly impossible! Fortunately, we're seeing an increasing number of small or boutique smokeries that use curing and smoking to showcase the individual virtues of the fish being used. This is akin to the way different kinds of feed and pasture are used to enhance lamb, poultry, pork, and beef. (More on this when we come to farmed vs. wild fish species.)

Smoke—the other seasoning for smoked fish—can be equally problematic or unwieldy, or wielded all too heavily. There are of course different smokes for different folks. There are those who favor a hearty, smoky flavor, while others incline toward a lighter, more nuanced approach. There are different smokes for different fishes as well. The final result of using a particular wood or blend of woods for smoking can be influenced by various things other than the fish itself: the wood species or variety (e.g., white vs. red oak) or the way the wood has been processed and how "clean" it is, meaning, how free of bark or other contaminants that can cause bitterness or oiliness. Hardwoods such as oak, beech, and some maples generally give a light clear smoke; fruitwoods such as apple, pecan, or peach can provide a smoky aromatic with a sweet mellowness; pear can be smokier still. Cherry can vary considerably, and while it is a good choice for game it is usually too strong and sharp for most seafood, though it seems to do well with things like mussels. Alder, the smoking wood of the Pacific Northwest, provides a heartier smokiness, closer to hickory but without the bitterness or heaviness this can often yield. Blends of hardwood and fruitwood, with a bit of hickory or alder, can give a nice complex smokiness without being overpowering. Evergreen woods are rarely used in this country for fish smoking, although a sprig or two in the mix can add a light, piney, herbal finish.

Finally, as mentioned previously, smoking can be "hot" or "cold," each process leading to completely different results in terms of flavor, texture, and types of use on the table. Cold-smoked fish have a supple, moist, easily sliced thin consistency—think classic smoked salmons from Ireland, Norway, Scotland, even the United States. Hot-smoked fish are usually cold-smoked for a period after curing; then the smoking continues at a low cooking temperature until the fish is flaky textured, easily flaked or chunked but not to be thinly sliced.

All this is simply to provide a starting point for talking about the various smoked fishes available at the market or from individual producers or purveyors. These products are the star ingredients for the recipes to follow.

Varieties of Smoked Seafood

Salmon

From whole poached salmon with fanciful garnishes centerpiecing an elegant buffet table to fish cakes from the can, salmon has long occupied a somewhat schizophrenic position on the culinary scene, spanning haute to everyday ho hum. The situation is similar for salmon's cured and smoked incarnations as well. Once represented in the United States by Pacific salmon heavily salted to palatability as "lox" for European immigrants on the East Coast, or hard-smoked almost to jerky on the West Coast, cold-smoked salmon morphed into more delicately cured and smoked Atlantic salmon, novie lox from Nova Scotia and New York smokehouses, and at the more exotic end the smoked salmons from England, Scotland, Ireland, and Norway. Thin, translucent slices of this salmon—draped or curled or furled—came to be an almost mandatory signifier of elegant dining and entertaining, and still hold sway even among recent challengers such as foie gras and truffles.

Hot-smoked salmon, a more traditional treatment in the Pacific Northwest and Alaska, has not enjoyed quite the same status, although with new approaches and seasonings, and growing interest in things ready to eat, that appears to be changing, here and abroad. Both cold- and hot-smoked salmons are now available from commercial-scale and specialty or boutique U.S. producers. Many are fairly recent newcomers that join a few long-standing New York/Brooklyn and West Coast institutions.

One development that has made year-round smoked salmon a possibility has been the rise of salmon farming in Europe, in Chile, and on both coasts of the United States and in Canada. From the beginning, salmon farming has sparked controversy along various lines. In the past five years this has become more heated as the industry expanded and as wild-salmon fisheries felt the commercial pressures accompanying this growth, with the resulting lower prices and year-round availability. In the United States, the controversy has been fueled significantly on the West Coast in Alaska, where wild-salmon runs support a viable commercial fishing industry and figure importantly in the way of life in many areas. On the East Coast, as elsewhere, the absence of reliable and sizable runs of wild salmon has no doubt undercut some of the vehemence brought to the cause on the West Coast.

There are five different kinds of wild salmon along the West Coast: the king, or chinook, the largest of the five and the most successfully promoted and marketed over the past twenty years; the sockeye; the coho, or silver; the pink; and the chum (the last two figure prominently in the canned-salmon-as-commodity industry, and the chum is a prime source of the salmon roe much prized in Japan). King salmon has been farm raised on a limited basis along the Pacific Northwest coast (but certainly not in Alaskan waters), and in Tasmania. The far and away dominant salmon species used in farming operations is the North Atlantic salmon, *Salmo salar,* which is a completely different species from the Pacific varieties. The North Atlantic salmon is the salmon of novie lox and European cold-smoked salmon fame. While there are still several sizable runs of wild North Atlantic salmon, such as the one fished off the Irish coast, most have been virtually nonexistent since the beginning of the twentieth century. Once so plentiful that New England servants complained about having to eat it daily, the North American salmon has virtually disappeared, with pollution of its spawning rivers most frequently identified as the likely culprit.

Like most controversies, the farmed-salmon debate is based on important economic interests. In the mid-1980s a marketing campaign to promote the wild king/chinook Copper River Alaskan salmon run took off, with a reprise each spring in anticipation of the run. In the past five years, and often at about the same time of year, farmed salmon has been under attack for various reasons, including contaminated feed, coloring agents with possible health implications, harboring of parasites that can possibly be spread to wild salmon species, and adverse effects on the local marine ecology. Some of these complaints are valid and deserve the attention the industry has in general afforded them. There is, for example, a movement in Europe toward certified organic farmed salmon, raised according to protocols that address problems of feed, farm siting, stocking densities, and ecological soundness. In addition, there are farms in other areas that are not certified as organic but whose practices and locations pass muster. In other words, not all salmon farms are the same.

An important aside on the question of farmed fish: trout, char, sturgeon, catfish, halibut, tilapia, and more recently cod are being farmed in the United States and Europe, and more exotic species are being farmed in Japan, in the Mediterranean, around Hawaii, and Down Under. Many of these, such as trout, sturgeon, and tilapia, are raised in closed systems, not in open-water pens, and so do not pose the ecological problems associated with salmon. And, often, there are no commercially available or viable wild-caught alternatives.

For lovers of the silky, delicate, cold-smoked salmon, this is a ray of hope, since the North Atlantic salmon is far and away *the* fish of choice for this product, due to the level and distribution of oils in its flesh. And while the farmed version of North Atlantic salmon may not achieve the heights of taste and texture of the wild North Atlantic, farmed North Atlantic salmon far exceeds what can be done with the Pacific varieties. (For the hot-smoked product, this is not necessarily the case.) Both cold- and hot-smoked salmon, whether North Atlantic, king, or sockeye, are extremely versatile as the basis of appetizers or canapés, in salads or entrées, with pasta, or in wraps or rolls. They can be turned into smooth or chunky spreads with few additional ingredients very easily.

Trout

Smoked trout, most commonly farm-raised rainbow trout widely available in boneless fillet form and hot-smoked, can develop a fine, rich flavor that stands up to mustards or even horseradish and is set off nicely with peppery greens or sweet bell pepper. While whole, bone-in smoked trout may well be the moist, full-flavored pinnacle for this fish, fillets are for most folks less daunting. They are easily used in salads or appetizers and make an excellent base for spreads.

Mackerel

While highly prized fresh or smoked in the United Kingdon and northern Europe, in the United States with few exceptions the mackerel is considered a trash fish, associated with the very worst connotations of "fishy," unlikely to be viewed as acceptable food, much less a gourmet treat. This was not always the case, as anyone who has had the good fortune to peruse Howard Mitcham's *Provincetown Seafood Cookbook* can tell you. Perhaps mackerel's sin was being plentiful and cheap. When properly caught and handled, mackerel is fine eating, and it is superb smoked. Its full flavor goes well with mustard or horseradish sauces, and smokehouse seasonings of herbs or pepper set it off quite nicely. Smoked whole on the bone, mackerel is almost spreadably smooth and unctuous, a far more subtly flavored delicacy than its Rodney Dangerfield reputation would suggest.

Bluefish

The East Coast bluefish is held in high regard and is worth seeking out both fresh and smoked. One might also call bluefish the East Coast equivalent of the Great Lakes whitefish—a seasonal tradition associated with vacations near or on the water. Like mackerel, bluefish is known as a strong-tasting fish, certainly not a white bread sort of flavor. Freshly caught and properly filleted, bluefish is actually far more delicately flavorful than most people are aware. Grilled or baked it makes good eating, and smoked it has a sturdy taste and texture that are well accompanied by whole-grain mustards. It makes superb spreads as well, with seasonings otherwise associated with *pâté de campagne*. It is generally a bit firmer and chewier than mackerel, with which it shares an affinity with mustards, horseradish sauces, black pepper, and fresh tomatoes. It is also amenable to various spreads or pâté preparations, and very good with salads and potatoes.

Sable

One of the most oil-enriched fish species, sable, or black cod, usually comes from frigid northern Pacific and Alaskan waters. Once sufficiently plentiful to be a staple of New York City tenement life, sable has been highly prized in Japan and more recently has become an almost cliché feature of white tablecloth restaurants in the United States. Smoked hot or cold, sable has a compact, silky texture and light flavor while simultaneously offering mouth-filling richness. Its oils seem to saturate all of the flesh, rather than being differentiated from the sable's lean flesh. James Beard described it as "gelatinous," perhaps not the most endearing culinary epithet. When smoked, sable hovers between cold- and hot-smoked in texture, thinly sliceable with a barely discernible, just emergent flake separation in the flesh. Sable can also be saltier than other smoked fish. Because it is usually hot-smoked at a very low temperature to prevent it from becoming flaky, sable requires more salt to prevent bacterial growth at smoking temperatures. Fresh sable, seared and baked in a hot oven to just-doneness, has the richness of foie gras; much of this is preserved in the properly smoked version, making it a luxury that is nicely set off with crisp textures and acidic or fruity flavors.

Sturgeon

An ancient species, and once so prevalent in the Great Lakes that it was given away free in bars as "Albany Veal," sturgeon has been fished almost to extinction for its roe in waters once largely under the control of the former Soviet Union. Several species are farmed here and in Europe, and wild sturgeon are caught along the Pacific Northwest coast. Meaty but mild in flavor, sturgeon can be cold- or hot-smoked. When adroitly handled, sturgeon is acclaimed by many to be one of the finest seafoods. Farmed "white" sturgeon in the United States is more lightly flavored than the wild.

Whitefish

Native to North American freshwater lakes from the Great Lakes northward, the whitefish is fairly light in flavor despite its relatively high oil content. Whitefish is smoked whole at a dwindling number of small smokehouses dotting the Great Lakes coastline. Familiar to New York City deli-goers, it is often made into smoked whitefish salad. When you can get whitefish freshly caught and smoked, it's a treat.

Catfish

Once associated, to its detriment, with fishing on the Mississippi, catfish is now widely available farmed from southern states. Improvements in feed and in pond construction have eliminated the muddy, grassy flavors that many people still instantly assume constitute the taste of catfish. Catfish has a firm texture and sweet flavor, and while its culinary uses are generally under the heading of "fried," it can be hot- and, perhaps more surprisingly, cold-smoked with extremely good results, the sweetness of the fish marrying well with the smoke. Smoked catfish is excellent in chowders or seafood stews, and it can play a very respectable stand-in for smoked cod or haddock in various dishes.

Haddock/Cod/Hake/Pollack

Major food fish from the North Atlantic, for Europe and North America, these are mild-flavored, low oil content species that flake easily when cooked. Smoked haddock is featured in traditional dishes of the United Kingdom, while salt-cured and air-dried cod are important preserved forms from Scandinavia to the Caribbean and across Europe, with an array of imaginative uses in Spain, Portugal, Italy, and France. Haddock, cod, hake, and pollack can be cured and smoked with splendid results and in turn can be used in a variety of cooked preparations, in many cases substituting for the salt-cured or air-dried forms in purees or brandades, fritters, chowders, stews, or fish cakes. Smoked pollack is a bit firmer and drier than the other three, but it is relatively abundant and reasonably priced—perhaps best suited to chowders and seafood stews where a range of textures is welcome.

Tuna

Like cod, tuna has been cured with salt and sun/air drying in warmer climates around the Mediterranean. Tuna is a muscular, fast swimming fish. Some tuna cuts are extremely lean and can be firm and dry when smoked; the fattier belly flesh of some tuna species can be cured and cold-smoked to a moister, more supple texture.

Scallops

Three varieties of scallop are generally available in the United States—"cisco" bay scallops, genuine "bay" scallops, and sea scallops. Cisco scallops are small, relatively less expensive, widely sourced, fairly chewy, and not at the high end of flavorful. In my experience, they account for most of the smoked scallops on the U.S. market and can in good condition provide a pleasant appetizer or salad garnish. Genuine bay scallops, available in variable abundance and during a season that can stretch from November into March but is often far more limited, are most closely associated with Nantucket, Martha's Vineyard, and Cape Cod. These are small but usually a bit larger than the ciscos, and they are incredibly sweet and flavorful. They can be eaten raw or very lightly sautéed, and smoking them would constitute a crime against nature and good taste. Sea scallops vary greatly in source, size, and flavorsomeness—when in good season, condition, and hands, they can be extremely tasty. They are also extremely delicate or fragile, in terms of longevity for peak flavor. During the holidays, when they will be enjoyed within a couple of days out of the smoking kiln, we cold-smoke largish (12- to 16-count per pound) sea scallops, which can then be sliced and eaten almost sashimi-like or very quickly seared with a still cool center and eaten as is or with some edgy greens. Unlike the cisco bays, unfortunately, good sea scallops, fresh or smoked, are priced in the special treat category for most of us.

Mussels

Mussels are widely available from farmed sources in the United States, Canada, New Zealand, and elsewhere. Farmed, they are generally clean of sand and beards and monitored carefully for possible pollutants. Smoked, a process they take to quite nicely, mussels are fairly widely distributed frozen, and properly handled they can be a fine addition to salads, risottos, and pasta dishes, or simply consumed "neat" with crackers. While I once considered tinned smoked mussels, perhaps from Korea, packed in, of all things, cottonseed oil, something of a treat, I've since renounced this part of my Midwestern culinary heritage and stick with what's on offer at the local reputable fish shop.

On the Platter and
Other Starters

Minimal Assembly Required

This is where we channel Elizabeth David. Smoked fish lends itself so well to quick, impromptu improvisations based on what other ingredients are fresh to hand and what you're in the mood for. So what follows are not really recipes so much as the kinds of ideas and suggestions my customers and I have shared over the years about "what to do with smoked fish."

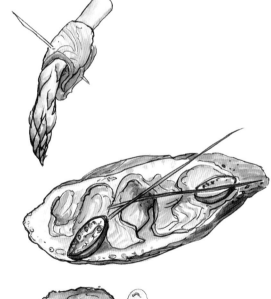

a favorite Ann Arbor restaurant, Café Zola, features a bruschetta—the famous tomato and grilled-bread appetizer that has launched a thousand variations—with Trackle-ments' smoked salmon, and many of the smokery's customers have offered both raves and variations on their version. These may be prepared with large slices of bread or with smaller cracker-sized cocktail-style servings. A good baguette, classic or sourdough, works for either size: for larger servings, slice baguette at a sharp angle for elongated ovals; for smaller servings, slice across at right angle to length. Slices can be grilled over charcoal, in a grill pan on the stove top, or in a panini-style electric grill.

Smoked-Salmon Bruschetta with Horseradish Cream

Crème fraîche, cream cheese, Greek yogurt, or mascarpone with grated fresh or prepared horseradish to taste

Toasted bread slices

Thinly sliced smoked salmon, in strips or squares to fit bread slices

Chopped chives, about ¼- to ½-inch lengths, or diced cherry or grape tomato

Kosher salt and freshly ground black pepper

Spread horseradish mixture on toasted bread slices; top with desired amount of smoked salmon. Sprinkle with chives or diced tomato. Season with salt and pepper to taste.

Smoked-Salmon Bruschetta with Tomato and Avocado

Hass avocado, ripe but not overly soft, peeled, diced

Diced cherry or grape tomatoes as needed, or Roma tomato, seeded, deveined, and diced

Smoked salmon, in ⅛- to ¼-inch dice

Dash of fresh lemon juice

Freshly ground black pepper

Slices of baguette or sourdough farm bread, grilled to light char marks

Toss avocado, tomato, and smoked salmon together; dress with lemon juice and black pepper to taste. Spoon over grilled bread slices. Or, layer sliced avocado topped with smoked salmon on bread slices and garnish with diced tomato.

Avocado does right by smoked salmon, its buttery richness standing in for cream cheese, or, well, butter. The Hass avocado with its high oil content is a good choice for this and other pairings with smoked salmon. For example, smoked-salmon tartare in avocado halves, with its evocation of guacamole, aptly suggests serving with corn tortilla chips, whether the chips are freshly made or from a bag (the blue corn variety provides a nice color contrast). Here, a fine dice of grape or cherry tomatoes provides an acidic offset to the combined richness of avocado and smoked salmon. Lemon or lime juice blended with crushed avocado works as well, as does a dash of a fine, brightly sharp vinegar such as the *agretto santo* style from Chianti or the amazing late-harvest moscatel vinegar available from Morgan & York here in Ann Arbor. An equal volume of smoked salmon and avocado is a good starting point, with half as much diced tomato.

Smoked Salmon on Rye Toasts with Cucumber and Red Onion

These can be done in large or small format, the larger more like the Danish *smoresbrød* open-faced sandwiches, the smaller a perhaps more familiar canapé style. For the larger size, use a good rye or a pumpernickel bread. For Trackle-ments' platters we use a hearty caraway rye or the lighter, sweeter onion or Jewish ryes from Zinger-man's Deli up the street or their pumpernickel, sliced to order. For smaller sizes, we quarter or halve the slices, depending on their size. Supermarkets often carry small presliced loaves of rye or pumper-nickel, or denser, more European-style, thinly sliced rectangular loaves. You can also lightly toast the thicker slices for a nice crunchy contrast with the softer bread inte-rior and the moist toppings.

> Rye or pumpernickel bread slices as needed
>
> Whipped cream cheese as needed
>
> Capers or caper berries, drained and rinsed (if using caper berries, slice into thin disks)
>
> 1 seedless cucumber, peeled if desired, thinly sliced on the diagonal and blotted dry with paper towels
>
> Thin-sliced smoked salmon as needed (4 ounces will be enough for 4 to 6 large toasts)
>
> Red onion, very thinly sliced, or scallion, white with a little of the green, split lengthwise and cut into ½-inch sections
>
> Freshly ground black pepper

Spread toasts lightly with cream cheese. Add capers or caper-berry slices to taste, top with cucumber, then smoked salmon. Garnish with onion. Season sparsely with black pepper.

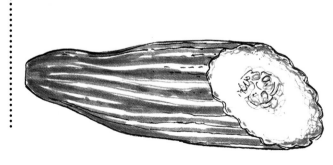

Cucumber Slices with Smoked Salmon, Pickled Ginger, and Chive

The green cucumber and chive set off the smoked salmon very nicely. Pickled ginger, the sort that is served with sushi, can be sandwiched between the cucumber and salmon, or placed on the salmon with ½-inch sticks of chive scattered on top. Four to 6 ounces smoked salmon, thinly sliced, will be enough for most of a whole cucumber.

Belgian Endive "Canoes" with Hot-Smoked Salmon or Trout

The slightly bitter, edgy taste and crispness of the endive leaves serve as a nice accompaniment and conveyance for rich smoked salmon or trout. If you wish, add a fine dice of cherry or grape tomato. A well-received variation on this at the smokery is made with our miso/mirin/tamari marinade–cured warm-smoked salmon, with just a slither of wasabi cream on the salmon (both Terrapin Ridge and Stonewall Kitchen brands of wasabi-lime or wasabi-mustard creams work well for this—use judiciously, especially the Stonewall Kitchen variety!).

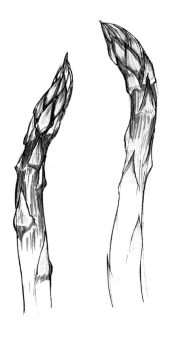

Blanched or Grilled Asparagus with Smoked Salmon

A very easy and tasty combination, with the crisp acidity of blanched or lightly grilled asparagus segments setting off the smoked salmon. Colors aren't bad either. Medium-thick asparagus is easiest to work with. Trim any hard, pale stalk off bottom. If blanching, cut into 1½- to 2-inch segments, toss into unsalted boiling water for a couple of minutes, and drain. If grilling, it's easier to work with whole spears, then cut into segments. Or, stir-fry segments briefly in a small amount of peanut oil with a dash of sesame oil. Trim thinly sliced smoked salmon into pieces that can be wrapped around asparagus with a bit of green showing at each end, and secure with a toothpick.

Avocado and Smoked-Salmon "Salsa" on Jícama Chips

Use just-ripe avocado, diced, dressed with fresh lemon or lime juice, a dash of olive oil, and a sprinkle of chili powder. Toss with flaked hot-smoked salmon or diced cold-smoked salmon and mound on thinly sliced jícama. If using hot-smoked salmon, mix very gently and briefly to avoid mashing the avocado and salmon together into a puree. Jícama provides a light, crisp, and juicy foil for the rich avocado/salmon mixture.

To prepare the jícama: peel deeply with a Y-peeler or square off all surfaces with a sharp knife. Slice into ⅛- to ¹⁄₁₆-inch slices, then cut the slices into about 1-inch by 1½-inch triangles or rectangles. Place in cold water laced with juice of lemon or lime and refrigerate until needed. Pat slices dry with towel before use.

Tricia's Inspiration

Serves 4

2 tablespoons light soy sauce

½ teaspoon sugar

¼ teaspoon sesame oil

16 to 20 asparagus spears (about 1 pound),
   trimmed, halved, and blanched

8 slices smoked salmon, about 1 by 2
   by ¼ inches each (about ¼ pound)

Toasted black sesame seeds as needed

Canned, drained mandarin orange slices as needed

Mix the soy sauce, sugar, and sesame oil together until well blended and sugar is dissolved. Dress the asparagus spears with the vinaigrette and lay them on a platter or on 4 individual plates. Strew the smoked salmon over the asparagus, sprinkle with black sesame seeds, and surround with mandarin orange slices.

Often on an appetizer platter you'll see asparagus spears wrapped inside prosciutto slices, bacon, or smoked fish. Here, it's "asparagus unwrapped" and simply dressed with a soy and sesame oil dressing. Beautiful and delicious.

Alycia's Smoked-Salmon Toasts with Cucumber and Greek Yogurt

Serves 6

This particularly refreshing take on bruschetta goes very nicely with a warm summer day and a chilled sauvignon blanc or soave.

6 slices baguette, ½ inch thick, sliced on diagonal

2 large cloves garlic, halved

Plain Greek yogurt or other plain yogurt as needed

18 cucumber slices, preferably English or seedless variety

½ pound cold-smoked salmon, sliced or diced

Minced chives or fresh lemon-thyme leaves as needed (optional)

Toast baguette slices lightly, then rub one side of each slice with the cut garlic cloves. Spread each toast with yogurt and top with cucumber and salmon. Garnish with minced chives or lemon-thyme leaves if using.

Smoked-Salmon Toasts with Egg Salad and Arugula

Serves 6

3 chilled hard-boiled eggs

¼ cup mayonnaise

1 teaspoon Dijon mustard

6 pieces diagonally sliced baguette,
    4 to 6 inches long, toasted

6 slices smoked salmon or equivalent, diced

Fresh arugula leaves as needed
    (whole if small, julienned if large)

Chop eggs, then toss with mayonnaise and mustard. Spread mixture on baguette slices. Top with smoked salmon and scatter arugula leaves over all.

Chopped hard-boiled egg is often presented with smoked salmon and/or caviar, along with red onion and capers. This version offers a nice contrast in texture and flavors and involves less dexterous handwork than smoked-salmon deviled eggs—and no worry about whether the egg whites tear.

Crispy Polenta Rounds with Smoked Salmon

Makes 8 appetizer portions

This is an easy way to combine the flavors of corn and smoked salmon, especially if you use the now widely available packaged, ready-to-use polenta. Chill the polenta before slicing into disks about ½ inch thick. The sugar and starch in corn work well with various smoked-fish preparations.

16 to 18 slices prepared polenta

Extra-virgin olive oil as needed

16 to 18 canapé-sized pieces of thinly sliced cold-smoked salmon

Freshly ground black pepper

Crème fraîche as needed (optional)

Sauté polenta slices over medium heat in olive oil until crispy and just browning at the edges. Transfer to a cooling rack over paper towels or to paper towels on a platter to drain. Allow to cool to room temperature, about 10 minutes. Place salmon slices on polenta slices and sprinkle with black pepper. To get some of the contrasting flavor sensations of a Baja-style fish taco, add a swatch of crème fraîche to the polenta before topping with the smoked salmon.

The Tracklements Grand Plateau

No seafood book would be complete without a *grand plateau de fruits de mer*. We first came upon this elevated platform of extravagance in the early 1980s at Le Congress, a steak and seafood restaurant in Paris. It is designed to fill you with awe and make you feel very privileged. A very large pizza pan, placed on top of a pedestal, is filled with crushed ice over which is arrayed all manner of seafood—oysters, clams, shrimp, lobster, crab. Smoked fish, especially salmon, bluefish, and mackerel, are perfect for this. Feel free to mix and match, you don't need the elevated pizza platter (any large platter is fine), and you can certainly live without the crushed ice. This is perfect for a special celebration and really must be accompanied by—depending on your budget after you've bought all this seafood—prosecco, cava, or champagne.

The Tracklements Grand Plateau, continued

Serves 12 to 16 (depending on appetizers and accompaniments such as crackers or bread)

Choose from and mix/match any of the following:

1 pound smoked salmon, sliced

1 smoked bluefish and/or mackerel fillet

1 pound shrimp, peeled and deveined

1 pound scallops, smoked or fresh and sautéed

1 lobster, cooked

1 pound crabmeat, preferably backfin, cleaned

1 dozen oysters or clams

1 pound mussels, smoked or steamed

Serve with one or more of the following condiments:

Tracklements Cocktail Sauce
Combine 1½ cups chili sauce and 1½ to 2 tablespoons minced ginger, to taste. This is fabulous with shrimp and clams, maybe even better than cocktail sauce made with horseradish.

Horseradish Sauce
1 cup light mayonnaise mixed with 1 to 2 tablespoons horseradish, to taste. Perfect on smoked bluefish and mackerel.

Grainy English Mustard
Also great on smoked bluefish and mackerel.

Mignonette
1 large or 2 small shallots, minced, stirred into ½ cup champagne vinegar or ginger/rice wine vinegar; for the oysters.

Preparation

Slice the salmon. Allow bluefish and/or mackerel fillets to come to room temperature. Boil the shrimp in water seasoned with peppercorns and Old Bay seasoning or with peppercorns, a bay leaf, ½ teaspoon thyme, and ½ teaspoon hot paprika. Drain shrimp as soon as they turn pink all over; do not overcook. Cool.

Scallops—one of the best ways to do these is to coat them lightly with ground *urfa* and *marash* peppers (moderately hot peppers from Turkey). Or use ground ancho or Anaheim chiles or any combination of chiles, hot, medium, or mild. Let scallops sit for about 20 minutes to slightly absorb the flavors of the peppers, then sauté in 1 tablespoon butter and 1 tablespoon extra-virgin olive oil over high heat just until they begin to develop fissures. Do not overcook. Remove from heat; cool.

Lobster—place lobster in soup pot with about 2 inches of boiling, lightly salted water, or ½ beer, ½ water, seasoned the same way as the water for the shrimp. Lobster is done when it has turned completely red and its tail is curled. Also important not to overcook. Let cool. Crack the claws, and split the tail.

Crabmeat—this is easy. Open the can, drain, check for cartilage, and array on a small plate.

Clams or oysters—if you can open these, it helps to put them in the freezer first for about 30 minutes and then open. If opening these is a challenge, see if the fishmonger or fish counter staff where you bought them will open them for you. While not as good as fresh, jarred oysters, especially in the fall and winter months, can be very good; you can lay them on some lettuce leaves and serve with the mignonette.

Mussels—Wash and debeard the mussels. In a large soup pot, sauté a medium onion, chopped, and 3 to 5 cloves of garlic, depending on your taste, in 2 tablespoons extra-virgin olive oil until the onion is translucent. Add 1 tablespoon thyme and a few grinds of black pepper. Pour in 2 cups dry vermouth or dry white wine, add the mussels, cover, and cook until they open. Remove to a plate; cool.

On the grandest serving platter you have, arrange the smoked fish and seafood you have chosen with the condiments nearby. Offer crackers or sliced baguette on the side. Open the bubbly and have a blast.

As with beef tartare, with salmon there's the question of which cut and how prepared. First, it's best to use an unsliced piece of smoked salmon rather than the thinly sliced variety. This can be cut into somewhat thicker slices or medallions, then julienned and chopped finely or coarsely for a superior texture and contrast with mix-ins. Use a knife to cut the salmon (you can put pieces in the freezer for 20 to 30 minutes to firm up, making slicing a bit easier). If you're using a whole piece of salmon, pieces from the collar (head) end and center cuts will be a bit richer with oils than those from closer to the tail end, which will have a firmer, leaner, and more uniform texture. The belly portions will be more buttery and richer. You may have an opportunity to mix trim from the belly and tail ends for a very affordable yet luxurious version. The proportions of mix-ins may be varied to balance with the differences in these cuts if you wish.

Smoked-Salmon Tartare I

Makes 20 pieces

6 to 8 ounces smoked salmon, in 1 piece, skin removed

2 tablespoons chopped chives

6 caper berries, stemmed, minced

1 tablespoon fresh lemon juice

Freshly ground black pepper

Crackers, toasts, seedless cucumber slices, or Belgian endive leaves

Slice smoked salmon into strips, julienne into ⅛-inch strips, then dice strips into ⅛-inch lengths or finer. Toss diced salmon with chives, caper berries, and lemon juice. Season to taste with a grind or two of black pepper. Serve on crackers, toasts, cucumber slices, or endive leaves.

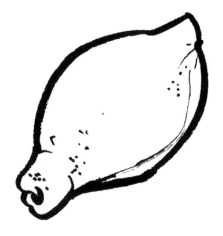

Smoked-Salmon Tartare II

Makes 20 pieces

6 to 8 ounces smoked salmon, in 1 piece, skin removed

3 scallions, white ends with some green, sliced lengthwise and then sliced thinly across

1 tablespoon light soy sauce or tamari

1 tablespoon rice-wine vinegar

¼ teaspoon brown sugar

Dash of sesame oil, or 1 teaspoon toasted sesame seeds

1 tablespoon minced daikon or water chestnut (optional)

Rice crackers

Julienned shiso leaves or watercress as needed

Slice smoked salmon into strips, julienne into very thin strips, then dice strips into equally thin lengths or finer. Mix together scallions, soy sauce, vinegar, sugar, and sesame oil or seeds. Toss together with salmon. Option: add a tablespoon or so of minced daikon or water chestnut. Serve on rice crackers with shiso or watercress.

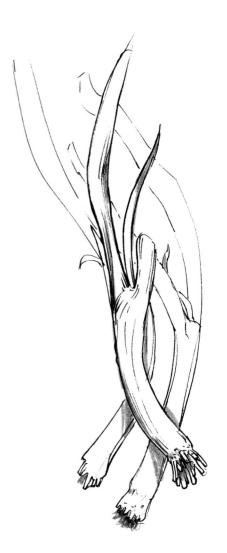

33

Smoked-Salmon "Pinwheel" Wraps with Lavash and Mascarpone

Makes about 48 pieces

This is an easy-to-prepare, visually arresting, and tasty concoction that invites tinkering with the final garnish.

4 10-inch lavash rounds, spinach or plain

4 to 6 ounces mascarpone

12-ounce piece smoked salmon, cut into 8 to 10 slices

Minced chives, arugula, watercress, or shiso leaf

Freshly ground black pepper

Wasabi cream or pickled ginger (optional; see note)

4 sushi-rolling mats

8 small rubber bands

Spread each lavash round almost to the edge with mascarpone, then place a layer of thinly sliced smoked salmon over the mascarpone. Top with herb or herbs of choice to taste. Sprinkle with black pepper. To add some extra zip, put a line of pickled ginger or wasabi cream across the lavash close to the edge you start rolling from, so it will be in the middle when finished. Roll tightly into a cylinder, wrap with a sushi-rolling mat, and secure with rubber bands at each end. Refrigerate for an hour or so to set. Remove rubber bands and rolling mat and with a sharp knife slice into ½-inch segments, arranging these on a platter with the interior "pinwheel" up.

Note: Ready-made wasabi cream is available in specialty and gourmet shops. To make your own, mix wasabi powder to taste with sour cream to desired heat.

Chunky Smoked-Trout Spread

Makes about 2 cups

6 to 8 ounces boneless smoked-trout fillet,
   skin removed and coarsely chopped

½ sweet red, orange, or yellow bell pepper,
   seeds and veins removed, finely diced

4 scallions, white part with a little green,
   finely chopped

1 tablespoon fresh lemon juice, plus
   more as needed

¼ teaspoon dried thyme or
   ½ teaspoon minced fresh thyme

Freshly ground black pepper

¼ cup Dijon mustard, plus more as needed

Dash hot-pepper sauce to taste (optional)

Mayonnaise (optional)

Sliced baguette rounds or celery sticks (see note)

Mix trout, bell pepper, and scallions together; add lemon juice, thyme, and a few grinds of black pepper. Blend in the Dijon mustard, adding more mustard if necessary just to moisten the whole mixture. Add hot-pepper sauce to taste if using. Taste and add more lemon juice if desired. If using mayonnaise, add a little at a time to desired consistency. Serve with baguette rounds or in celery sticks.

Note: A good substitute for sliced baguette, here as elsewhere, is the water cracker, which has a more flaky than crunchy texture, true bite-sized diameter, and a lighter flavor with less salt.

Hot-smoked salmon and other fish such as trout, mackerel, and bluefish can be flaked, not sliced, for similar preparations. Mixing the flaked fish with the spreads in advance can make it easier to assemble the finished piece and finesse the possibility that the flaky bits might fall off. Smoked mackerel and bluefish, in particular, can stand up to a higher proportion of mix-ins and creams used as binders. The same is true of many commercially available hot-smoked salmons, as these can be a bit heavy on the smokiness. It's best to taste the smoked fish on its own to assess both smokiness and saltiness before proceeding. What sets this recipe apart from the usual spreads is the use of mustard sauces as the principal moistener and binder, with the option of adding a small amount of mayonnaise, mascarpone, or cream cheese to smooth out the spread, or to add a bit of sweetness to balance the mustard's acidity. Neither smoothly blended spread nor tossed "salad" mix, this spread shows off each ingredient alongside the others in appearance and taste. The Dijon mustard dressing, just enough to bind ingredients together, is sufficient on its own, but the addition of mayonnaise extends and slightly sweetens the whole.

The preceding trout recipe can be used with either smoked mackerel or blue-fish, with additional bell pepper and scallion. Here is a different version that draws on the fish cookery of Kerala, India.

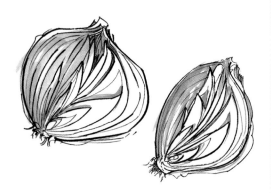

Smoked-Bluefish Spread

Makes about 2 cups

6 to 8 ounces smoked bluefish or mackerel, skin removed and coarsely chopped (see note)

¼ red onion, finely diced

4 new potatoes, fingerlings, or small Yukon golds, cooked but still firm

¼ teaspoon good curry powder

1 tablespoon fresh lemon juice

Mayonnaise as needed

Baguette rounds or crackers

Toss all ingredients except mayonnaise and baguette slices together. Add mayonnaise a little at a time to desired consistency. Serve with baguette rounds or crackers.

Note: East Coast smoked bluefish can be quite salty; additional potato and mayonnaise can offset this. Taste and add if desired.

Smoked-Salmon Tortillas

Serves 6

8 ounces cold- or warm-smoked salmon

2 ripe avocados, peeled, pitted

6 flour or corn tortillas

1 cup low-fat sour cream or plain Greek yogurt

Chopped scallion, minced fresh or pickled jalapeño
  pepper, and cilantro or parsley leaves as needed

For those avoiding the carbs of bagels but still wanting a special Sunday brunch treat, try this simple combination.

Slice the salmon and avocado in strips. Cover the stack of tortillas with a damp paper towel and microwave for 30 seconds to warm, or warm on a griddle or skillet. Place the warm tortillas, the salmon, avocado, and sour cream or yogurt on the table and let everyone build their own brunch tortillas. Garnish each with scallion, jalapeño, and cilantro or parsley. Excellent with mimosas.

Pita Bread with Greek Yogurt and Smoked Salmon

Makes 8 to 12 slices

This dish sounds deceptively simple, but don't pass it over. It's luscious as an appetizer or light lunch.

2 9-inch pita loaves, or 1 12-inch lavash

2 to 4 cloves garlic, crushed

2 tablespoons tahini (optional)

2 teaspoons ground cumin

1 tablespoon extra-virgin olive oil

1 cup plain Greek yogurt

4 to 6 ounces cold-smoked salmon, sliced

½ cup toasted pine nuts

Heat the bread in a 400°F oven or toaster oven until it is warm and just starting to crisp. Meanwhile, whisk the garlic, tahini, cumin, and olive oil into the yogurt. When the bread is done, put on a platter, top with the yogurt mixture, then the sliced salmon, and finally the pine nuts. Slice into wedges and serve.

Vietnamese Spring Rolls

Makes 16 rolls

½ cup Thai fish sauce

1 tablespoon sugar

1 tablespoon grated fresh ginger, or to taste

1 teaspoon chili paste with garlic

2 cups uncooked rice vermicelli

1 cup seeded, julienned cucumber,
and/or 1 cup peeled, julienned daikon

8 scallions, white part with just a bit of
the green, cut into 2-inch lengths and
sliced lengthwise

2 cups shredded lettuce

16 rounds of 8-inch-diameter rice paper

½ cup each whole fresh mint, basil,
and cilantro leaves

6 ounces hot- or cold-smoked salmon,
cut into 2-inch julienne, about ¼ to ½ inch thick

These are beautiful, elegant, healthy, lo-cal, and fun to make. In fact, you can prepare the ingredients in advance and have guests help make them as you sip wine before dinner. Also, you can choose what you'd most like to put in each, and guests can custom make their own.

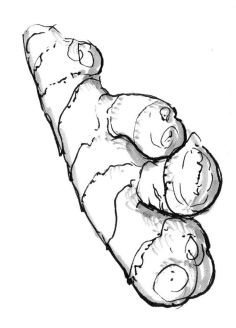

For the dipping sauce: Whisk together the fish sauce, sugar, ginger, and chili paste. Reserve. For the filling: Put the uncooked rice vermicelli in a bowl and cover with boiling water. Stir and let sit until vermicelli softens. Drain vermicelli and chop coarsely into 2-inch lengths or so. Fold vermicelli, cucumber, scallions, and lettuce together gently to mix. Fill a deep-dish pie plate, large enough to hold the rice paper, with hot water. Place a sheet of rice paper in the water and as soon as it softens remove to a plate or flat surface. Lay a mint leaf in the middle of the bottom third of the rice paper, followed by 2 or 3 slices of salmon. Lay on about 2 tablespoons of the vegetable/vermicelli mixture. (Do not use more than about 2 tablespoons of stuffing in each roll.) Top with 1 each basil and cilantro leaf. Fold the bottom edge over the stuffing, then fold in the sides. Roll up to close and lay seam down on a serving platter. Repeat until all the rolls are done. Serve with the reserved dipping sauce.

Thai Fish Cakes

Makes about 8 1½-inch cakes

Fish cakes are a classic treat in Thailand. These fish cakes, made with smoked salmon, haddock, or cod, not only have a smoky edge, they're as good as in the restaurants.

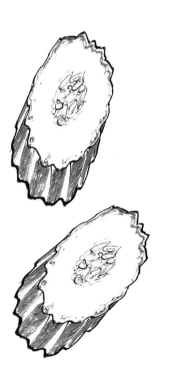

Cucumber Sauce

3 tablespoons white-wine or rice vinegar

3 tablespoons sugar

4 tablespoons water

1 small cucumber, peeled, seeded, quartered lengthwise, and sliced

2 tablespoons minced ginger

1 Serrano chili, seeded and minced

Few flakes dried red chili pepper

1 tablespoon chopped cilantro

Fish Cakes

4 ounces white fish, such as tilapia, wolffish, or farmed catfish, cut into cubes

4 ounces smoked salmon, haddock, or cod, cut into cubes

2 tablespoons red curry paste (see note)

1 egg, slightly beaten

1 teaspoon sugar

3 tablespoons fish sauce

Grated zest of 1 lime

2 tablespoons finely chopped raw green beans

Canola or other vegetable oil as needed

For the sauce: Combine the vinegar, sugar, and water in a small saucepan and simmer until sugar has dissolved. Let cool, then stir in the remaining ingredients. Reserve.

For the fish cakes: Combine both fishes, curry paste, and egg in food processor. Whisk sugar into the fish sauce; when dissolved, add to the processor and blend into the fish mixture. Transfer to a bowl and mix in the lime zest and the chopped green beans. Form into small cakes and fry in oil on both sides until lightly browned. Serve with the cucumber sauce on the side.

Note: Red curry paste is available in many Asian markets.

Moroccan Fish Cakes

Makes about 15 1½-inch cakes

This recipe is inspired by Claudia Roden's wonderful cookbook *Arabesque,* which covers Moroccan, Turkish, and Lebanese cuisine. The smoked fish gives these cakes extra depth. A wonderful appetizer.

½ pound white fish, such as cod, haddock, wolffish, or farmed catfish, skinned, boned, and cut into cubes

½ pound smoked cod or haddock, cut into cubes

1½ teaspoons ground cumin

¼ teaspoon smoked paprika (see note)

3 cloves crushed garlic, or to taste

1 egg, beaten lightly

Grated zest of 1 lemon

½ cup chopped cilantro

Canola or other vegetable oil as needed

Flour for dredging

½ cup plain Greek yogurt mixed with 2 cloves finely minced garlic

Put the fishes in a food processor along with the cumin, paprika, garlic, egg, lemon zest, and cilantro and combine until smooth. Do not overprocess. Fry a small piece of the mixture in a nonstick pan with a small amount of oil until brown on both sides. Taste and add kosher salt to uncooked mixture if needed. Form into 1½-inch cakes and dredge lightly in flour. Fry in oil until lightly browned. Remove from pan and drain on paper towels. Serve immediately with a small dollop of the yogurt mixture on the side.

Note: Smoked paprika is available at specialty markets and shops. See the Sources section on page 128.

Smoked-Salmon Cakes with Red-Pepper Sauce

Serves 4

½ to ¾ pound smoked salmon, skinned, minced

½ cup plain white dry bread crumbs

1 egg, lightly beaten

1 medium onion, finely chopped

1 large clove garlic, finely chopped

4 tablespoons chopped parsley

Juice of 1 lemon

Hot-pepper sauce to taste

Freshly ground black pepper

Vegetable oil as needed

1 lemon, cut into wedges

With a small amount of salmon and some readily available ingredients, this recipe transforms the entire concept of "fish cakes" as most of us have experienced them. Don't stint on the accompanying sauce, either. If you run out of cakes before the sauce is done, your guests will happily dunk chunks of bread, or their fingers, into the remainder with audible enjoyment.

Place salmon in bowl. Add remaining ingredients except the vegetable oil and lemon wedges, using a fork to mix. With your hands, carefully shape the mixture into 8 cakes. In a heavy skillet, heat enough oil to form a thin film on pan surface. Sauté the fish cakes about 3 minutes on each side, until they are golden brown and heated through. Garnish with lemon wedges and serve with Roasted Red-Pepper Sauce or a mayonnaise-based sauce of your choice.

Recipe continued on next page ⟶

**Smoked-Salmon Cakes
with Red-Pepper Sauce,
continued**

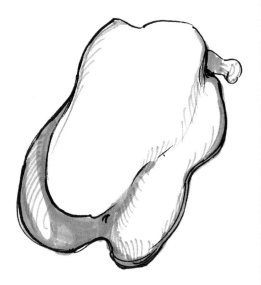

Roasted Red-Pepper Sauce

2 roasted sweet red peppers,
    or ¼ cup commercial sweet-red-pepper spread

¼ cup capers

4 tablespoons chopped parsley

Juice of ½ lemon

½ teaspoon finely chopped fresh
    hot chili pepper, or to taste

1 tablespoon mayonnaise

Peel and seed the sweet peppers and either chop to a paste or
purée in a food processor or blender. Mix the paste with the
remaining ingredients. If you are using the ready-made pepper
spread, simply mix it with the other ingredients. Cover
and refrigerate until ready to use.

Smoked-Salmon Dumplings with Meyer Lemon Vinaigrette

Makes about 20 dumplings

Peanut or other light vegetable oil as needed

1 package mascarpone (about 8 ounces)

Zest of 1 large lemon

1 large or 2 small bunches scallions,
  green and white parts thinly sliced on a long bias

Kosher salt

About 20 wonton skin squares

6 ounces Tracklements peppered miso mirin
  hot-smoked salmon or other hot-smoked or
  kippered salmon, broken up into chunks
  (about ¼ ounce each)

Light oil such as peanut or canola for frying

Heat oil in saucepan or deep fryer to 350°F. Place mascarpone, lemon zest, scallions, and a generous pinch of salt in mixing bowl, mixing together. Lay out wonton squares and place a scant teaspoon of mascarpone mixture on each square. Top with a chunk of smoked salmon and then top with another scant teaspoon of mascarpone mixture. One at a time, brush edges of wonton square lightly with water and then fold corner to corner to form a triangle. Dumplings should be plump yet easy to seal. After edges of dumplings have been pressed together, gently push any remaining air pockets out of filling and inspect edges for a good final seal. Fry dumplings in hot oil until just golden. Remove from oil; drain; sprinkle lightly with kosher salt. Serve immediately with Meyer Lemon Vinaigrette for dipping.

Recipe continued on next page ⟶

guest chef recipe

by Eve Aronoff

Eve Aronoff is the chef-owner of eve restaurant in Ann Arbor, Michigan. She is also the author of the cookbook *Eve*. Meyer lemons are sweeter and less acidic than regular lemons and well worth seeking out as a substitute.

Meyer Lemon Vinaigrette

2 shallots, minced

2 egg yolks

1 tablespoon water

¼ cup fresh Meyer lemon juice (or substitute regular fresh lemon juice if Meyer lemons are unavailable)

Zest of 1 lemon

½ teaspoon hot-pepper sauce

1½ teaspoons Shark brand sriracha (see note)

½ teaspoon kosher salt

½ cup light oil such as peanut or canola

½ cup extra-virgin olive oil

Place all ingredients except peanut and extra-virgin olive oils in food processor. Turn processor on and add oils in a slow, steady stream until emulsified.

Note: Sriracha is hot-pepper sauce from Thailand. It can be found in Asian and other specialty markets.

Recipe courtesy of Eve Aronoff.

Smoked Mackerel with Daikon, Mizuna, and Mâche Salad with Yuzu and Miso Vinaigrette

Serves 4

12-ounce piece smoked mackerel

For the salad

1 ounce daikon, cut into 2½-inch julienne

1 ounce carrots, cut into 2½-inch julienne

¼ ounce pink radish, cut into paper-thin slices

1 ounce daikon or other radish sprouts

1 ounce Belgian endive, julienned

½ ounce mizuna or arugula, washed and dried

½ ounce mâche, washed and dried

Lightly toss daikon, carrots, pink radish, and sprouts together in bowl. Reserve. Toss endive, mizuna, and mâche in bowl. Reserve.

Recipe continued on next page ⟶

guest chef recipe
by Takashi Yagihashi

Takashi Yagihashi is the former executive chef at the internationally renowned Tribute in Farmington Hills, Michigan; former executive chef at Okada at Wynn Las Vegas; and chef-owner of Noodles in Chicago. This recipe is a study in contrasts of taste and texture, pairing the richness of mackerel with the crunch of radish, carrot, and endive and the tart notes of yuzu and rice vinegar.

Yuzu and Miso Vinaigrette

¼ cup yuzu juice (or substitute ½ fresh
   lime juice, ½ fresh lemon juice; see note)

¼ cup rice vinegar

¼ cup sweet yellow miso (see note)

¼ cup grape seed oil

1 teaspoon sesame oil

1 teaspoon soy sauce

1 teaspoon sesame paste or tahini

½ teaspoon sea salt

¼ teaspoon freshly ground black pepper

Mix all ingredients in bowl, whisking slowly. Reserve or refrigerate until ready to use. (Can be made ahead and refrigerated 1 week.)

Note: Yuzu, an Asian citrus, is available in Asian markets. Yellow miso is available in Asian and Japanese markets.

Lotus Root Chips

1 quart vegetable oil

16 paper-thin slices of fresh, peeled
   lotus root

¼ cup cornstarch

1 teaspoon sea salt

1 tablespoon toasted black sesame seeds

Heat oil to 300°F. Lightly coat lotus root slices with cornstarch. Deep-fry lotus root about 4 to 5 minutes or until crispy and golden brown. Drain on paper towels and season with sea salt while still hot. Let cool to room temperature. Reserve.

Shiso-Leaf Oil (optional)

36 shiso leaves (see note)

2 cups grape seed oil

Bring 1 quart water to a boil. Add shiso leaves and cook 5 seconds, stirring. Strain immediately, then plunge into ice water. Allow leaves to chill. Using cheesecloth or terry towel, squeeze as much water as possible from leaves. Place grape seed oil in blender with shiso leaves. Puree leaves thoroughly. Strain oil through fine mesh. Refrigerate until ready to use (may be made several days to 1 week ahead).

Note: Shiso leaves (also called oba) are available in Asian food markets.

Presentation

Slice mackerel into 12 roughly equal-size pieces. Divide salad into 4 portions, placing each on a rectangular plate. Place 3 slices mackerel on top of each salad portion. Then place vegetable mixture on top of mackerel. Arrange vegetables in the same direction as the shape of the mackerel (not crosswise).

Place lotus root chips on top of vegetable mixture. Drizzle 1 teaspoon vinaigrette on lotus root chips (off center). Drizzle 1 teaspoon optional shiso-leaf oil over salad and fish. Finish with a sprinkle of toasted black sesame seeds on top. Repeat this procedure for each serving.

Recipe courtesy of Takashi Yagihashi.

Smoked Salmon and Salmon Roe on Crispy Potato Pancakes with Horseradish Cream and Pickled Onions

Serves 4

1 large baking potato

2 tablespoons unsalted butter

2 tablespoons vegetable oil

Kosher salt to taste

½ cup crème fraîche or sour cream

1 tablespoon fresh lemon juice

1 tablespoon grated fresh or drained bottled horseradish

Freshly ground black pepper to taste

2 ounces smoked salmon, julienned

1 tablespoon caviar or salmon roe

½ cup pickled red onions (recipe follows)

Peel and coarsely grate the potato. Working in batches, heat butter and oil in large nonstick skillet over medium-high heat until very hot. Sprinkle 2 tablespoons of potatoes into pan, pressing into a 3-inch diameter with spatula to create lacy, flat rounds of potato. (Don't be concerned if you can see the bottom of the pan through gaps in potato.) Cook until well browned, pressing down firmly, 5 to 7 minutes per side. Season with salt while hot. Cakes can be made several hours in advance and crisped in hot oven before serving.

Combine crème fraîche, lemon juice, and horseradish in small bowl. Season with salt and pepper. Arrange 3 pancakes per serving on small plates. Top pancakes with equal amounts smoked salmon, a spoonful of horseradish cream, and a spoonful of caviar. Top with a few pickled onions and serve. *Recipe continued on next page* ⟶

guest chef recipe

by Sara Moulton

Sara Moulton often makes these at home for special occasions when the family is together. Sara and her husband Bill load them up with "the works." Assuming you also want the works, you'll appreciate the way that the crisp and salty potato pancakes complement the richness of the salmon and caviar. The pancakes should be almost as thin as potato chips. To get them that thin, spread them out in a nonstick pan and press them down. The pickled onions are a wonderful sweet-and-sour addition.

**Smoked Salmon and
Salmon Roe on Crispy
Potato Pancakes,
continued**

Pickled Red Onions

2 medium red onions, sliced ¼ inch thick

1½ cups cider vinegar

2 garlic cloves, peeled and halved

3 tablespoons sugar

1 tablespoon pickling spice

1½ teaspoons kosher salt

Combine onions, vinegar, garlic, sugar, pickling spice, and salt in small saucepan. Bring to a boil over high heat. Reduce heat to medium; simmer 2 minutes. Remove from heat; cool to room temperature before serving. Chop fine. Pickled onions last for a week in refrigerator.

Recipe courtesy of Sara Moulton, from Sara Moulton Cooks at Home *(New York: Broadway Books, 2002).*

Salads Cold and Warm

Tomato, Chickpea, and Smoked-Salmon Salad

Serves 4

This salad is a wonderful surprise, filled with different colors, tastes, and textures—it could be a meal in itself!

1 pint grape tomatoes, halved

1 large cucumber, peeled, seeded, and diced

1 bunch scallions, chopped into disks

1 can chickpeas, drained (or substitute canned black or cannellini beans)

Chopped cilantro

For the dressing

2 to 3 cloves garlic, minced

1 tablespoon sherry vinegar

4 tablespoons extra-virgin olive oil

Kosher salt and freshly ground black pepper

4 ounces smoked salmon, sliced into thin strips (or substitute smoked cod, trout, or haddock)

Combine the tomatoes, cucumber, scallions, chickpeas, and cilantro to taste in a bowl. Whisk the dressing ingredients together and add to the vegetables. Add salt (sparingly) and pepper to taste. Arrange salad on 4 plates. Lay the strips of salmon on top and serve.

White Bean Salad with Smoked Salmon

Serves 8

2 cups dried white beans or
   2 15-ounce cans small white beans

8 cups cold water

2 bay leaves

2 cloves garlic

6 to 8 ounces smoked salmon, diced

4 tablespoons extra-virgin olive oil

2 tablespoons fresh lemon juice

Freshly ground black pepper

½ cup chopped parsley

Bring beans and water with bay leaves and garlic to boil for 2 minutes; set aside, cover, and let stand 1 hour. Bring back to boil, reduce heat, and simmer until beans are completely cooked but not falling apart, about 1½ hours. Let cool; then drain and rinse with cold water. If using canned beans, drain in colander and rinse with cold water and add 1 pressed garlic clove to dressing.

Add smoked salmon, olive oil, lemon juice, and black pepper to taste. Toss lightly and refrigerate until thoroughly chilled to blend flavors. Warm to room temperature before serving. Sprinkle with chopped parsley.

Variation: Substitute quartered, boiled, chilled new potatoes for the beans and smoked trout for the salmon if desired.

Roasted Golden Beets with Smoked Fish

Serves 4

olden beets—beautiful, delicious, and easy to prepare. Pair them with smoked mackerel or smoked salmon for a very different and elegant salad or appetizer.

1 to 2 tablespoons extra-virgin olive oil

1 pound stemmed golden beets

2 cloves garlic, crushed

1 teaspoon Dijon mustard

1 tablespoon white-wine vinegar

4 tablespoons blood-orange olive oil
  or a good extra-virgin olive oil (see note)

4 ounces smoked mackerel or smoked salmon,
  lightly flaked or thinly sliced

Preheat oven to 400°F. Coat a cast-iron skillet or roasting pan with olive oil, roll the beets in the oil, and then bake in the oven for 1 hour or until a fine skewer or knife passes easily in and out of them. Remove from oven. While beets cool, make the dressing by mixing together the crushed garlic with the mustard and vinegar. Using a whisk, beat in the oil. Reserve dressing. Once the beets are cool, peel them and slice into disks. Drizzle the dressing over the sliced beets and top with the smoked fish.

This salad can be made ahead and kept covered and chilled until shortly before serving.

Note: Blood-orange olive oil may be purchased online from Stonehouse Olive Oil of California (see Sources section on page 128).

Tortellini Salad with Smoked Salmon

Serves 4

9 to 10 ounces fresh cheese tortellini

2 tablespoons extra-virgin olive oil

¼ cup chopped fresh dill

½ cup thinly sliced scallions (optional)

3- to 4-ounce piece smoked salmon,
matchstick julienne

For the dressing
Combine ¼ cup olive oil, 2 teaspoons Dijon mustard,
2 tablespoons fresh lemon juice, and freshly ground
black pepper to taste.

In 3 quarts of boiling water, cook tortellini to al dente.
Drain thoroughly. Toss with olive oil, dill, and optional scallions. Add salmon and dressing; toss just
until thoroughly coated. Can be served immediately
but benefits from sitting at least 2 hours, refrigerated.
Bring to room temperature before serving.

This particular recipe is drawn from *Gorky Park*, in a scene at the Russian Tea Room in New York where grilled gravlax is served. Turns out that this is a traditional way of preparing cold-smoked salmon in Scandinavia and northern Europe. The appeal of this approach has been reinforced by customers at the smokery who reported, to my surprise, that they always grill the cold-smoked salmon outside over charcoal or inside on a George Forman or panini-type grill. A similar approach is simply to sear the salmon in a skillet over medium heat in olive oil. Since the salmon is cured, the texture is firmer than grilled fresh salmon, and the curing and smoking add complexity to the taste. After grilling, let the salmon come to room temperature before assembling with greens and serving. This approach works better with cold-smoked fish that are oil rich, such as salmon or sable, not so well with something like haddock (finnan haddie). Large, cold-smoked sea scallops do very nicely too.

Grilled or Sautéed Cold-Smoked Salmon or Gravlax, with Arugula and Romaine

Use about 4 ounces of cold-smoked salmon per serving, in 1 piece, preferably skin-on center cut from the fillet, lightly brushed with olive oil. (Spraying the grill or grill pan with Pam or other nonstick spray helps prevent sticking.) Start skin side down, about 2 minutes; turn; and repeat. If you have a rectangular hamburger or hot dog grill basket sprayed with Pam, it's much easier to manage the grilling and turning without risk of breaking up the fish. The nonstick Forman or panini grills, with top and bottom cooking surfaces, are even easier.

Place grilled or seared salmon pieces on arugula or romaine lettuce and serve with lemon wedges or a mustard vinaigrette.

Seared Smoked Sea Scallops with Greens and Vinaigrette

Smoked scallops as needed (see note)

Assorted greens of choice (see note)

For the vinaigrette

2 parts oil to 1 part vinegar

½ teaspoon Dijon mustard per ½ cup of finished vinaigrette

Kosher salt and freshly ground black pepper—go very lightly on the salt as the smoked scallops add their own

If using a good champagne, sherry, moscatel, or Chianti vinegar, you could skip the oil and opt for the mignonette version. Stir together finely minced shallots with your choice of vinegar and some freshly ground black pepper. A splash of champagne or Riesling won't hurt at all. This is also a superb accompaniment to freshly shucked oysters or littleneck clams.

For the oil, use an extra-virgin olive oil, or 1 part walnut oil to 3 parts canola or safflower oil. Use a good rice vinegar or champagne vinegar. There are some very nice white vinegars from the Chianti region, and a late-harvest moscatel vinegar that's astonishingly good on salads with or without seafood, and perfect for a mignonette as well (available from Ann Arbor's Morgan & York; see the Sources section, page 128). Blend the mustard with the vinegar and salt and pepper to taste. Whisk in the oils until smooth (omit mustard if using walnut oil version). Dress the greens with the vinaigrette, place salad on plates, and top with scallops.

Note: Most smoked scallops commercially available are hot-smoked bay scallops, which also go well with mixed greens. Cold-smoked sea scallops, which are much larger and have a silkier, less chewy texture, can be sliced into medallions and scattered over mixed greens with a light vinaigrette, for a "crudo" approach. But, as with the grilled or sautéed cold-smoked salmon, searing the cold-smoked scallops adds color and a bit of crustiness, while preserving the delicate interior. Use scallops that are 12 to 16 count per pound, 2 scallops per serving. Any of the baby greens now available work well. Adding a bit of sliced endive leaf adds crunchiness and sharpness, and fresh watercress provides a hint of lemon.

Seared Cold-Smoked Sable or Black Cod with Greens and Vinaigrette

For this preparation, use 2 to 3 ounces sable—very rich!—per serving. With its high oil content, cold-smoked sable (black cod) has more the texture of a cold-smoked sea scallop. The flavor is quite delicate, but the textural richness is the thing here. Sear the fish very quickly in a lightly oiled skillet or on the grill, no more than a couple minutes per side. Let cool, slice into medallions, and serve with greens and vinaigrette as in the preceding recipe for Seared Smoked Sea Scallops with Greens.

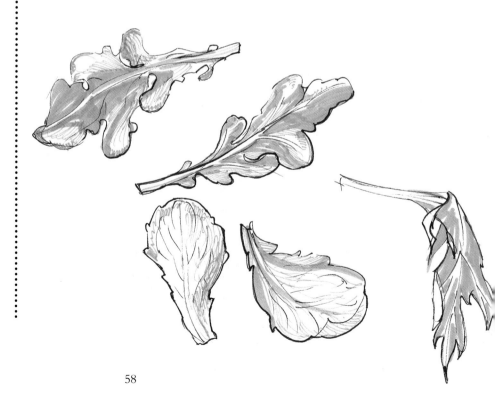

Salade Niçoise with Smoked Mackerel, Bluefish, or Trout

Serves 2

4 to 6 ounces of smoked fish
(about 1 boneless fillet of mackerel or trout)

4 to 6 small red new potatoes, cooked, chilled

8 to 12 good-sized green beans, blanched
3 to 4 minutes in boiling water, chilled

12 cherry or grape tomatoes, halved

2 slices of red onion, halved and separated

Lettuce greens as needed

2 tablespoons extra-virgin olive oil

1 tablespoon white-wine or champagne vinegar

½ teaspoon Dijon mustard

Kosher salt and freshly ground black pepper

On an attractive platter, assemble smoked fish and vegetables in whatever fashion you'd like on a bed of lettuce greens. Mix olive oil, vinegar, mustard, and salt and pepper to taste until well blended and drizzle over all. Serve immediately.

Greens or green beans, cherry or grape tomatoes, sliced boiled potato, slivers of red onion—all set off the rich flavor of these hot-smoked fish. For variety and additional color, slices or julienne of cold-smoked salmon can garnish this dish, replacing anchovy in the classic version.

Arugula and Snow-Pea Salad with Smoked Salmon

Serves 6

This salad can be made with smoked bluefish or mackerel, flaked into salad greens before dressing. Add halved grape or cherry tomatoes for extra color and bite.

2 tablespoons fresh lemon juice or white-wine/champagne vinegar

2 teaspoons extra-virgin olive oil

Freshly ground black pepper

4 cups loosely packed arugula

4 ounces snow peas, trimmed

½ cup peeled, thinly shaved celery root or jícama (optional)

4 to 6 ounces smoked salmon, sliced thin or julienned

Whisk together lemon juice and olive oil with a grind or two of pepper. In large salad bowl, toss arugula, snow peas, and optional celery root or jícama with smoked salmon. Add dressing. Toss well and serve immediately.

Smoked-Trout, Cucumber, and Radish Salad with Cilantro Cream

Serves 6

3 fillets good-quality smoked trout, about 4 ounces each

1 English cucumber, sliced into half-moons

½ small sweet onion (Vidalia or Walla Walla), thinly sliced

6 large red radishes, thinly sliced

2 tablespoons thinly sliced cilantro leaves

¼ teaspoon ground cumin

½ teaspoon sea salt

Freshly ground black pepper

½ teaspoon grated lemon zest

1½ tablespoons low-fat plain yogurt

For the cilantro cream

1 cup low-fat plain yogurt

2 tablespoons chopped cilantro

1 teaspoon grated lemon zest

Freshly ground black pepper

6 teaspoons trout caviar

guest chef recipe
by Susan Goss

Susan Goss is the executive chef and co-owner of the popular West Town Tavern in Chicago, where they smoke their own trout for this salad. Trout caviar is available from several online sources such as Zabar's and Browne Trading Company. See Sources section on page 128.

Break each trout fillet into large pieces. Set aside. In large bowl, combine cucumber, onion, radish, cilantro, cumin, ½ teaspoon sea salt, pepper to taste, lemon zest, and yogurt. Mix well. Reserve salad at cool room temperature while making the cilantro cream. To make the cilantro cream: in blender jar combine yogurt, chopped cilantro, lemon zest, and pepper to taste. Puree until very smooth. To serve, toss smoked trout with cucumber salad and divide among 6 chilled plates. Drizzle cilantro cream over trout and around salad. Top each salad with 1 teaspoon trout caviar.

Recipe courtesy of Susan Goss.

guest chef recipe

by Mario Batali

Mario Batali is not only a brilliant chef, he's also a household word. Mario has appeared on Food TV in his own program, as well as making guest appearances on the wildly popular *Iron Chef*. Batali owns several restaurants and shops, including Babbo, Lupa, Esca, and Otto Enoteca Pizzeria, and is the author of numerous cookbooks. This recipe features smoked sable, which was on the first menu at Batali's restaurant Babbo. Like all Italian recipes, it is simplicity—and sublimity—itself.

Smoked Sable "Carpaccio" with Citrus Salad and Da Vero Olive Oil

Serves 4

1 pound smoked sable, very thinly sliced

2 blood oranges, cut in segments

1 grapefruit, cut in segments

Juice of 1 lime

Leaves from 1 bunch flat-leaf parsley

½ cup Da Vero or other excellent quality, boutique olive oil, plus more for drizzling

Kosher salt and freshly ground black pepper to taste

Overlap several slices of sable on each of 4 chilled dinner plates. In medium bowl, combine the orange and grapefruit segments, lime juice, parsley, olive oil, salt, and pepper, and toss well. Divide the salad evenly among the 4 plates. Drizzle with the juices remaining in the bowl and a bit more oil. Serve immediately.

Recipe courtesy of Mario Batali, from The Babbo Cookbook *(New York: Clarkson Potter, 2002).*

Soups

New England Smoked-Fish Chowder

Serves 6

This is an excellent, hearty, and easy-to-make soup and is always a crowd pleaser. You can make the base hours or even a day ahead of time and then add the potatoes and fish just before serving. The soup will be thick with fish and potatoes, almost like a stew.

6 ounces bacon, cut into 1-inch squares

1 tablespoon extra-virgin olive oil

4½ cups sliced onions

2 tablespoons flour

3 cups chicken stock, warmed

1 to 2 teaspoons dried thyme

2 bay leaves

1 cup clam juice

½ cup dry white wine or vermouth

3 to 4 cups thinly sliced baby red potatoes

Kosher salt and freshly ground black pepper

1½ pounds smoked haddock, cut into 1-inch cubes

1 pound other white fish, such as hake, tilapia, or cod, cut into 1-inch cubes

12 to 24 shucked oysters (optional)

Parsley as needed

Sauté the bacon in the olive oil in an 8-quart soup pot on low heat until the bacon has rendered its fat and is cooked through but not crisp; do not brown or burn. Add the onions and cook on low heat, approximately 7 to 10 minutes, stirring occasionally, until they are wilted and very lightly browned. Add the flour and mix in well; cook another 2 minutes. Pour in the warmed chicken stock, add the thyme and bay leaves, and stir well with a wooden spoon to mix in with the flour. Add the clam juice and wine and stir to mix. Cook, covered, on low heat for 10 to 15 minutes. Add the sliced potatoes and cook just until they are tender but still have a slight crispness; they should not be falling apart. Season to taste at this point with salt and pepper. Add the smoked and fresh fish and cook just until the fish is opaque. If using oysters, add 30 seconds before serving; stir and cook 30 seconds. Garnish with parsley.

Mediterranean Chowder with Smoked Haddock and Scallops

Serves 6

1 medium red onion, coarsely chopped

1 green bell pepper, chopped into ½-inch dice

2 tablespoons extra-virgin olive oil

4 to 5 cloves garlic, minced

2 bay leaves

1 teaspoon smoked paprika (see note)

¼ teaspoon ground allspice

2 cups chicken broth

2 cups clam juice

1 28-ounce can crushed tomatoes

½ cup dry white wine

½ pound chorizo, andouille, or high-quality kielbasa (peeled if desired), diced

Kosher or sea salt and freshly ground black pepper

1½ pounds smoked haddock

½ pound white fish such as tilapia, cod, or wolffish

Smoked scallops (if available)

Bunch of cilantro, stemmed and chopped

Recipe continued on next page ⟶

This chowder draws from Spanish, Moroccan, and Portuguese traditions. If you can get smoked scallops they are an excellent addition, but the soup is also delicious without them. The base can be made hours or even a day ahead of time, and you can then add the fish just before serving.

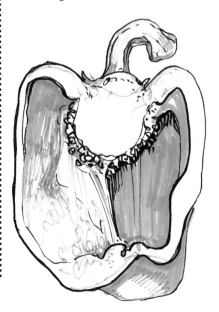

Mediterranean Chowder with Smoked Haddock and Scallops, continued

In an 8-quart soup pot sauté the onion and bell pepper in the olive oil over medium-low heat until they soften and the onions become translucent, about 6 to 8 minutes. Add the garlic and cook for another 30 seconds, letting it cook slightly but not brown. Add the bay leaves, smoked paprika, and allspice. Mix well and cook for another 2 minutes. Add the broth, clam juice, tomatoes, and wine. Stir until well blended, then cook, covered, on low heat for 20 minutes. Add the sausage and continue cooking, covered, for another 10 minutes. Season to taste with salt and pepper. Add the fish and cook just until translucent. If using smoked scallops, add 30 seconds before serving. Garnish with chopped cilantro.

Note: Smoked paprika, a distinctly flavored condiment from Spain, is completely different than Hungarian-style sweet paprika. It can be purchased in specialty food shops and online. See Sources section on page 128.

Asparagus Velouté with Smoked Salmon

Serves 4

2 tablespoons extra-virgin olive oil

1 medium onion, coarsely chopped

1 to 2 leeks, well cleaned, white portion with some green, thinly sliced

1 pound asparagus, ½ inch trimmed off ends if dry

1½ cups chicken stock, preferably homemade

Heavy cream (optional)

¼ pound cold-smoked salmon, julienned or diced

Warm oil in soup pot. Add onion and leeks; cover and cook gently over low heat until soft but not browned. Add asparagus, cover, and continue cooking about 10 minutes. Add chicken stock, bring to a simmer, and cook for 15 to 20 minutes or until asparagus is cooked through and soft. Place soup mixture in food processor and blend to a puree. (For added textural elegance and ultrasmoothness put soup through a sieve, food mill, or chinois.) If desired, float a tablespoon or so of heavy cream on top of the soup or stir in completely until you get the color and texture you like. The velouté may be served warm or cold. Room temperature is fine. Serve in small cups garnished with smoked salmon.

OK, this isn't a classic velouté in the sense that Julia would approve. In fact, I associate the basic technique with something my good friend Eric would throw together when we were in graduate school. His version rested heavily on broccoli stalks and perhaps some cauliflower. At that time, most asparagus came in cans, and if it didn't we certainly couldn't afford it. And smoked salmon just never came into the picture. Here the soup is thickened with only the pureed vegetables. A dash of cream or half-and-half to finish and enrich is acceptable.

Corn Chowder with Smoked Fish

Serves 6 to 8

1 yellow onion, about 8 ounces, diced

1 sweet red bell pepper, seeded and diced

2 tablespoons canola or corn oil

1 teaspoon ground cumin seeds

1 teaspoon ground coriander seeds

3 cups fresh or frozen corn kernels

1 pound Yukon gold or russet-type potatoes, peeled and diced

4 cups chicken stock

1 poblano pepper, roasted, peeled, seeded, and diced

1 cup cooked black beans (canned are fine), drained

1 pound hot-smoked salmon, or cold-smoked haddock, cod, or catfish (see note)

Chopped scallions or chives as needed

In 4- to 6-quart soup pot, sauté onion and bell pepper in oil until they soften, 8 to 10 minutes. Add ground spices, then corn kernels, potatoes, and stock and bring to boil, cooking for 10 minutes or so, or until the potatoes are done. Reduce heat to simmer. Mash some of the corn and potatoes to thicken the stock to desired consistency. Add poblano, beans, and fish. Simmer chowder 3 to 4 more minutes. Chowder may be served immediately, garnished with scallions or chives. Or cool, cover, refrigerate, and reheat just before serving.

Note: If using cold-smoked fish, poach fish 3 to 4 minutes in a mixture of equal parts simmering milk and water to cover. Remove and add to pot at the same time as the corn and potatoes.

Portuguese Caldo Verde with Smoked Fish

Serves 6 to 8

1 pound smoked cod, haddock, hake, or catfish

Milk as needed

1 large yellow onion, minced

2 garlic cloves, minced

3 to 4 tablespoons extra-virgin olive oil

6 large russet potatoes, peeled and thinly sliced

2½ quarts water

4 to 6 ounces linguiça or chouriço, sliced thin, sautéed, and drained on paper towels (optional)

1 pound fresh collard, kale, or chard, stemmed and sliced very thin

Freshly ground black pepper

Simmer fish to cover for 3 to 4 minutes in a mixture of equal parts milk and water. Drain, cool, and flake. Reserve. In a 4- to 6-quart pot sauté onion and garlic in olive oil over medium-low heat until onions turn translucent, about 8 to 10 minutes. Add potatoes and sauté another 4 to 6 minutes, stirring. Add water, bring to boil, then simmer until potatoes are fall-apart tender, about 20 to 25 minutes. Remove pot from heat and mash potatoes into the water with a wooden spoon or manual potato masher until soup is desired consistency. Add sausage if using and simmer another 5 minutes. Add greens and simmer another 5 minutes. Just before serving, add reserved poached fish and season to taste with black pepper.

Along with *sopa de coentro* (fresh coriander soup), this soup was a lunchtime favorite of my wife Susan and me in the restaurants along the Atlantic Ocean breakwater at Caparica, not far across the bridge from Lisbon. Traditionally made with linguiça or chouriço, this version with smoked white fish can heartily hold its own in any season. Add pan-fried thin slices of the sausage if you wish—you won't be sorry! In Portugal, the green (*verde*) is provided by the leaves of a local cabbage. Here, a good substitute is collard or turnip greens, kale, or chard.

Smoked-Salmon Chowder

Serves 4 to 6

This is a variation on salmon chowder using smoked salmon and adding a little bit of heat with a poblano pepper and, if you choose, chipotle.

1 medium onion, halved and sliced

1 medium poblano pepper, halved and sliced

2 tablespoons extra-virgin olive oil

2 tablespoons butter

2 tablespoons flour

4 cups hot fish stock, or 3 cups chicken stock and
   1 cup lobster or fish stock

2 tablespoons fresh dill, chopped

1 teaspoon chipotle (optional)

1 medium russet potato, peeled, halved, and sliced

1 cup fresh or frozen, thawed, corn kernels

12 ounces hot-smoked salmon, diced or
   broken into pieces

2 tablespoons sherry

In a large soup pot, sauté the onion and poblano in the olive oil and butter until softened. Add the flour and stir in to mix evenly. Sauté lightly several minutes. Whisk in the stock until smooth, then add dill and optional chipotle. Add the potatoes and cook until just tender (don't overcook or they'll fall apart). Add the corn and cook about 1 minute, then stir in the salmon and the sherry just until the salmon is warmed through. Serve immediately.

Thai Bouillabaisse with Smoked Haddock

Serves 4 to 6

1 large onion, chopped

2 to 3 tablespoons vegetable oil

1 stalk lemongrass, chopped

3 tablespoons minced ginger

1 to 2 teaspoons red-pepper flakes

4 to 6 cloves garlic, minced

1 14-ounce can coconut milk

2 teaspoons red chili paste

2 teaspoons tamarind paste

3½ cups chicken stock

1 14-ounce can chopped tomatoes

¼ cup fresh lemon juice

2½ tablespoons sugar

3 tablespoons Thai fish sauce

3 tablespoons chopped fresh basil

1 pound smoked haddock, chopped into 1-inch cubes

16 mussels

1 pound shrimp, peeled and deveined

Chopped cilantro as needed

This is a sensational Thai version of the classic bouillabaisse, with the unexpected twist of smoked fish. The base can be made hours or even a day ahead of time and the fish added just before serving.

Sauté the onion in the oil over low heat until translucent. Add the lemongrass and ginger and sauté for 1 minute, then add the red-pepper flakes and garlic, cooking for 30 seconds, until the garlic releases its flavor but is not browned. Add the coconut milk, then stir in the chili and tamarind pastes. Stir to blend well. Add the chicken stock and tomatoes, followed by the lemon juice, sugar, and fish sauce. Cook, covered, over low heat, for 15 minutes. Add the chopped basil and cook 10 more minutes. Add the fish and cook for 1 minute, then add the mussels and cover. When a third of the mussels have opened, add the shrimp and cover. As soon as all the shrimp turn pink and the mussels have opened, ladle into bowls and sprinkle with cilantro.

Harira

Serves 6

I was introduced to harira by the fabulous *Moro* cookbooks of Samuel and Samantha Clark. Harira is traditionally a lamb soup from Morocco, and it is heavenly in the fall and winter. This is a lighter version, topped off with smoked cod or haddock. It's very easy to make and a real crowd pleaser.

1 large onion, finely chopped

3 celery ribs, finely chopped

2 tablespoons extra-virgin olive oil

3 to 5 garlic cloves, or to taste, minced

Large pinch saffron

½ teaspoon ground cinnamon

½ teaspoon turmeric

½ teaspoon ground ginger

¼ teaspoon ground cloves

8 cups chicken broth

⅔ cup lentils

¾ cup split peas

1 bunch cilantro, chopped

1 14-ounce can diced tomatoes

2 tablespoons chopped fresh oregano

1 bunch chard, leaves only, shredded, or 3 cups baby spinach

Juice of ½ lemon

Kosher salt and freshly ground black pepper

4 ounces smoked cod or haddock, coarsely chopped

Sauté the onion and celery in the olive oil until they soften and the onion becomes translucent. Add the garlic and stir in briefly, then add the spices until they are well mixed with the onions and celery and give off their aroma. Add the chicken broth, lentils, split peas, and about ¾ cup of the chopped cilantro. Cook about 30 minutes, or until the lentils and peas have softened. Add the tomatoes and oregano and once they have mixed in with the broth, add the chard or spinach and cook until it is well wilted. Add the lemon juice and season with salt (sparingly) and pepper to taste. Ladle into serving bowls and garnish with the smoked cod or haddock. Pass the remaining cilantro for garnish.

Indian Smoked-Fish Bouillabaisse

Serves 4

1 cup minced onion

½ cup minced celery

2 tablespoons extra-virgin olive oil

2 tablespoons minced ginger

3 to 5 cloves of garlic, minced

½ to 1 teaspoon hot pepper flakes,
   or to taste (optional)

1 teaspoon ground cumin

1 teaspoon ground coriander

½ teaspoon cinnamon

¼ teaspoon ground cloves

2 cups split peas

8 cups chicken broth

2 cups smoked cod or haddock,
   cut into 1-inch cubes

Cilantro leaves as needed

This delicious soup combines three things rarely put together—Indian spices, a Mediterranean style of soup, and smoked fish.

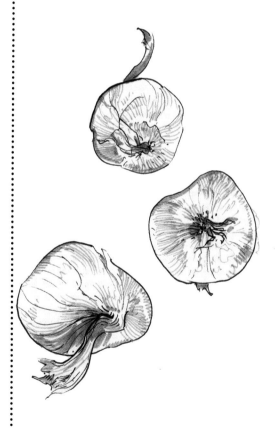

Sauté the onion and celery in the olive oil until they soften and the onion is translucent. Add the ginger and cook briefly, then add the garlic, stirring constantly. Do not allow garlic to brown. Add the spices and mix thoroughly with the vegetables. Add the split peas and stir just so they are coated with the spice mixture. Add the chicken broth and cook, covered, for 45 minutes to an hour until peas are soft. If you like your soup smooth, puree in batches in a food processor; if you like it chunky, serve as is or smash some of the peas against the side of the pot. Put ½ cup smoked fish in each of the 4 bowls; pour the hot soup over the fish and garnish with cilantro.

Seafood Chili with Smoked Fish

Serves 6

The chili base can be prepared well in advance—an overnight in the refrigerator helps mellow the chili flavors—and the final concoction put together shortly before serving. Smoked fish gives a depth of flavor customarily achieved only by adding the chipotle chili—a smoky dried jalapeño that carries a considerable heat.

Sauté onion and garlic in the oil over low heat until onions are translucent. Add the bell pepper and stir several minutes. Add tomatoes with juice. Add stock or bouillon and ground ancho chile, cumin, oregano, and coriander. Simmer on low heat 30 to 45 minutes. (If a thicker chili sauce is desired, add optional tomato paste at this point and blend in with liquid.) Twenty minutes before serving, add the smoked fish and simmer. Just before serving add the remaining fish and scallops, and continue cooking until firm, about 5 minutes. Garnish with chopped cilantro if desired and serve with crusty bread or over rice or pasta.

3 to 4 medium onions, chopped

4 garlic cloves, minced

2 to 3 tablespoons extra-virgin olive oil or corn oil

1 green or red bell pepper, cored and chopped

1 28-ounce can peeled whole tomatoes, quartered, with juice

4 cups fish stock, or 2 cups fish stock and 2 cups vegetable stock

2 tablespoons ground ancho chile or regular chili powder

1 tablespoon ground cumin

2 tablespoons dried oregano

1 tablespoon ground coriander seed

1 6-ounce can tomato paste (optional)

1 pound smoked white fish (cod, pollack, tautog, ocean catfish) fillets cut into 1-inch cubes

1 pound firm-fleshed white fish (monkfish, tautog)

½ pound bay scallops

½ cup chopped cilantro (optional)

Smoky White Bean Soup

Serves 6 to 8

1 large onion, diced

1 to 2 ribs celery, diced

1 carrot, diced

2 tablespoons extra-virgin olive oil

4 cloves garlic, minced

2 14½-ounce cans chopped tomatoes

2 tablespoons canned chipotles in adobo sauce

6 cups chicken, veal, or vegetable stock

2 cups water

¾ pound dried white beans or 2 15-ounce cans cannellini beans, drained

2 tablespoons chopped parsley

Kosher salt and freshly ground black pepper

½ to 1 pound smoked cod, haddock, or bluefish, cut or broken into bite-sized pieces, room temperature

Chopped cilantro (optional)

*W*hite beans and smoked fish are a match made in heaven, and this luscious soup combines the smoothness of the beans with the smokiness of chipotles and smoked fish. The chipotles also add some heat to make this mildly spicy; if you want it hotter, just add more chipotles. Cooking the dried beans in the liquid without the traditional presoak method means they absorb all the good flavors, but canned beans work well, too.

Sauté the onion, celery, and carrot in olive oil in a large soup pot until softened. Add the garlic toward the end of cooking and sauté just until softened. In a blender or food processor, puree the tomatoes and chipotles, then add to the vegetables along with the stock, water, beans, and parsley. Simmer, covered, until the beans are tender, about 1½ hours. (If you are in a hurry, you can eliminate the water, reduce the amount of stock to 4 cups, and simmer briefly until the flavors have mixed, about 20 minutes. Then add the drained, canned beans and proceed.) Once the beans have cooked, remove the soup from the heat and puree anywhere from half to a third of the soup in a blender or food processor and return to the pot. Season to taste with salt and black pepper. Serve the soup, each bowl topped with a small mound of the smoked fish and optional cilantro to taste.

Pasta, Rice, Potatoes, and More

Pasta, potatoes, rice, pizza—and don't forget cheese and eggs—
are quintessentially congenial to American ways with food—
economical, open to infinitely inventive variation, easily adaptable
to each season or occasion. Preparation is opportunistic,
exploiting whatever is ready to hand at the store, farmers'
market, or in the pantry or refrigerator.

Linguine with Smoked Salmon and Scallions

Serves 4

Basically a simple pasta with oil and garlic, this recipe demonstrates how easily a dish can be transformed by adding a small amount of smoked seafood, and how the seafood can serve as a foil against a garnish of green vegetable. The variations and improvisations that follow the recipe are limited only by what seems fresh and provocative at the market.

Variations and Improvisations

For the pasta

Spinach linguine for color
   contrast and flavor

Red-pepper linguine for flavor

Capellini or penne for texture

Additional vegetables

Sautéed spinach, chard, or radicchio

Steamed or sautéed asparagus
   tips or pieces

Tiny green peas or sautéed snow peas

Diced sun-dried tomatoes

---

2 tablespoons good-quality extra-virgin olive oil

3 to 4 cloves garlic, minced

¾ pound dry linguine

4 to 6 ounces smoked salmon (if available by the piece, slice into matchstick pieces; if presliced, cut into thin 1- to 1½-inch strips)

1 bunch scallions or Chinese leeks, sliced lengthwise to include some green, and cut into 1-inch pieces

Kosher salt and freshly ground black pepper

Grated Parmesan or pecorino cheese as needed

Bring 4 to 5 quarts lightly salted water to boil. Heat olive oil over low heat and add garlic, taking care not to burn it. Remove from heat. When water boils, add linguine and cook about 8 to 10 minutes. When pasta is almost done, return oil and garlic to low heat. Drain linguine in colander and place in serving bowl. Pour oil and garlic over pasta and toss to thoroughly coat. Add smoked-salmon strips and scallions and toss lightly. Serve immediately, seasoning to taste with salt, pepper, and grated cheese.

Meredith's Pasta with Smoked Salmon and Olives

Serves 4

2 shallots, minced

1 small onion, minced

1 clove garlic, minced

2 tablespoons extra-virgin olive oil

½ cup dry white wine or vermouth

½ cup clam broth or water

¾ pound dry pasta of choice
(cappellini, vermicelli, or other pasta)

½ cup crème fraîche or cream

15 small cured black olives, pitted,
rinsed thoroughly, and sliced or
coarsely chopped

½-pound piece smoked salmon,
cut into matchstick pieces

Kosher salt and freshly ground black pepper

Chopped parsley as needed

Freshly grated Parmesan or Romano cheese

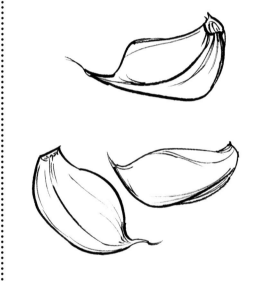

Bring 4 to 5 quarts lightly salted water to boil. Meanwhile, sauté shallots, onion, and garlic in olive oil until lightly browned. Add wine and cook over medium heat about 3 minutes. Add clam broth or water and cook 3 to 5 minutes more. At this point, add pasta to boiling water, stirring. Lower heat under broth mixture and whisk in crème fraîche. Add olives and cook 2 to 3 minutes. Check pasta for doneness and drain. Add smoked salmon to sauce and cook just until heated through. Season to taste with salt and pepper. Serve immediately over pasta with parsley and grated cheese.

Linguine with Smoked Mussels

Serves 4

This is a relatively straightforward preparation that gets a lot of extra mileage out of using smoked mussels. The version with smoked mussels seems more suited to the cooler seasons, with the mussels giving up more of their smokiness to the oil used to dress the pasta. From start to finish, this dish only takes about 30 minutes.

4 medium-sized shallots, minced

1 large clove garlic, minced

¼ cup extra-virgin olive oil

¾ pound dry egg linguine

1 cup smoked mussels, about 5 to 6 ounces (see note)

¼ cup chopped Italian parsley

Bring 4 to 5 quarts lightly salted water to boil. When water is about to boil, lightly sauté shallots and garlic in olive oil over low heat. Add linguine to the boiling water; cook until just tender, about 10 minutes. Drain pasta and place in serving bowl. Add mussels to the oil and shallot mixture to warm for a minute or so. Pour mussels over pasta and toss with the chopped parsley. Serve immediately.

Note: Smoked shrimps or scallops, or a combination of the two, may be substituted for the smoked mussels for a lighter smokiness concentrated more in the seafood than diffused in the dish and a firmer texture overall. Smoked oysters may also be used for a result more similar to that for mussels. Also, for variation in color and flavor, try substituting spinach pasta or sweet-red-pepper pasta for the egg linguine. Adding 4 to 5 tablespoons finely chopped red or yellow sweet pepper provides a counterpoint in texture and flavor as well as color. Peppers should be sautéed 3 to 4 minutes before adding to mussels.

Fettuccine Alfredo with Smoked Salmon

Serves 4

1 cup heavy cream

3 tablespoons butter

1 pound dry fettuccine

⅔ cup grated Parmesan cheese

4 ounces cold-smoked salmon, cut into 1-inch strips (see note)

Freshly ground black pepper

In a stainless steel, enameled, or other nonreactive pan large enough to hold the cooked fettuccini, simmer briefly together ¾ cup of the cream and the butter until the mixture thickens. Turn off the heat. Bring 4 quarts lightly salted water to boil, add the fettuccine, and return to boil. Cook approximately 8 to 10 minutes to desired doneness. Drain pasta and place in pan with the thickened cream and butter; toss over low heat, adding remaining cream, the Parmesan, smoked salmon, and several grinds of black pepper. Serve immediately.

Note: While this recipe calls for cold-smoked salmon, hot-smoked may also be used, resulting in a smokier flavor.

A simple and rewarding variation on a classic preparation. The addition of crisp baby peas or chopped red or yellow pepper provides a nice contrast to the salmon's smokiness and the creamy sauce. Many Tracklements customers have written to suggest variations on this use for leftover bits of both our Highland Smoked Salmon and our Mediterranean Smoked Salmon.

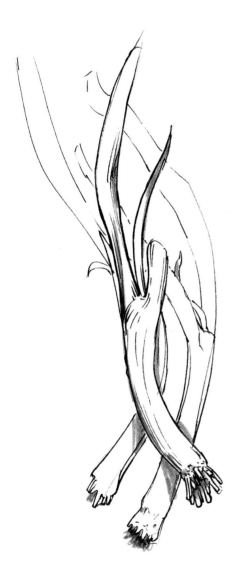

Pasta Primavera with Smoked Salmon or Trout

Serves 4

12 to 16 thin asparagus spears, trimmed, sliced diagonally into 1½-inch pieces

1 sweet red, orange, or yellow bell pepper, seeded and julienned

2 tablespoons extra-virgin olive oil

8 ounces dry bow-tie (farfalle) pasta

6 ounces smoked salmon, julienned into 1½-inch strips or 1 fillet (6 ounces) smoked trout, skinned and flaked

2 scallions, white with a bit of green, cut into 1-inch lengths, halved lengthwise and separated, or 6 to 8 fresh chives cut into 1-inch lengths

¼ teaspoon fresh lemon juice

Freshly ground black pepper (optional)

Sauté asparagus and peppers in olive oil about 3 to 5 minutes until tender and just beginning to brown. Remove from heat. Cook pasta in 4 quarts lightly salted boiling water about 10 minutes or to desired doneness. Drain and toss with asparagus and peppers. Add smoked salmon or trout, scallions, and lemon juice and toss together. Season to taste with black pepper if desired.

Penne with Asparagus, Smoked Salmon, and Sesame Seeds

Serves 4

12 asparagus spears, trimmed and sliced
    into 1- to 1½-inch pieces

8 ounces dry penne pasta

3 scallions or 8 fresh chive stems

2 tablespoons extra-virgin olive oil

2 teaspoons fresh lemon juice

6 to 8 ounces smoked salmon, julienned

1 to 2 tablespoons toasted sesame seeds

Freshly ground black pepper

Blanch asparagus pieces in lightly salted boiling water about 3 minutes. Drain and rinse under cold water. Reserve. Cook penne in 4 quarts lightly salted boiling water 10 to 12 minutes or to desired doneness. Drain but do not rinse. Reserve. Trim roots from scallions, leaving a bit of green on top. Halve lengthwise, then slice into 1-inch cross sections. If using chives, cut into 1-inch segments. Mix olive oil with lemon juice; pour over reserved penne along with asparagus, salmon strips, and sesame seeds. Season to taste with black pepper. Serve at room temperature or slightly chilled.

Fettuccine with Smoked Salmon, Arugula, and Endive

Serves 4 as a starter or light entrée

8 ounces thin to medium asparagus spears, trimmed and sliced diagonally into 1- to 1½-inch pieces

8 ounces dry fettuccine

4 tablespoons extra-virgin olive oil

2 small shallots, minced

2 heads Belgian endive, leaves separated and rinsed, thinly sliced crosswise

2 tablespoons fresh lemon juice

4 to 6 ounces cold-smoked salmon, cut into thin or julienned strips

Freshly ground black pepper

Blanch asparagus in boiling water 3 to 4 minutes. Drain and rinse under cold water. Reserve. Cook fettuccine in 4 quarts lightly salted boiling water about 8 to 10 minutes or to desired doneness. Drain but do not rinse. Reserve. Pour olive oil into 10-inch skillet, add shallots, and sauté about 2 minutes. Add endive and cook 1 additional minute. Remove from heat and add asparagus and lemon juice; stir together gently. Place fettuccine in warm serving dish or on platter and top with asparagus mixture. Lightly mix ingredients into pasta. Top with smoked salmon. Season to taste with black pepper.

Tortellini with Smoked Salmon and Dill

Serves 4

8 to 10 ounces fresh or frozen cheese tortellini

For the dressing

¼ cup extra-virgin olive oil

1 tablespoon fresh lemon juice

1 teaspoon Dijon mustard

½ cup scallions (with some of
the green tops) or chives, cut into
1-inch pieces

2 tablespoons chopped fresh dill

3 to 4 ounces cold-smoked salmon, cut
into strips or julienned, or same amount
hot-smoked salmon, flaked

Cook tortellini according to package instructions until pasta is just tender. Drain and place in warm serving bowl. Whisk together dressing ingredients and toss gently with tortellini, scallions, dill, and smoked salmon.

There are numerous recipes out there for pasta with smoked salmon garnished with grated cheese. This one has a distinct advantage in that the pasta separates the cheese and salmon into more distinct flavor-texture sensations.

Smoked-Salmon and Shrimp Ravioli

Serves 6 to 8

*E*veryone loves these elegant little raviolis made with wonton wrappers. They make a beautiful first course or lovely light dinner.

For the sauce

1½ tablespoons rice or champagne vinegar

1 teaspoon ground coriander

1 teaspoon pressed garlic

¼ teaspoon sugar

3½ ounces extra-virgin olive oil

Kosher or sea salt and freshly ground black pepper

¾ cup quartered grape tomatoes

¼ to ½ cup fresh basil leaves, loosely packed, chopped

½ pound shrimp, peeled and deveined

½ pound cold-smoked salmon

4 ounces light cream

1 tablespoon minced scallions or chives

48 wonton wrappers

1 egg white, lightly beaten

First, make the sauce. Combine the vinegar, coriander, garlic, and sugar in a small mixing bowl, then whisk in the olive oil. Add salt and pepper to taste. Combine with the tomatoes and basil and reserve.

Coarsely chop the shrimp and grind it together with the smoked salmon in a food processor. Add the cream and blend thoroughly. Place mixture in bowl and fold in scallions with a spatula.

Place a rounded teaspoonful of the salmon-shrimp mixture onto a wonton wrapper. Paint the edges of the wrapper with the egg white and press another wonton wrapper on top. Press the edges to seal so that the wonton looks like a small pillow. (Before finally sealing the wontons, be sure to remove as much air as possible from between them by gently pressing air bubbles out.)

Fill a low, 10- to 12-inch saucepan two-thirds full of lightly salted water and bring to a boil. Slip the ravioli in 2 to 3 at a time (don't overcrowd the pan) and cook until they come to the surface about 1 minute. Retrieve with a sieve or slotted spoon and place in a warm serving dish. Cover dish with foil while cooking remaining ravioli. Serve immediately with a drizzle of the sauce on top

Orecchiette and White Beans with Hot-Smoked Salmon or Cod

Serves 4

½ pound dry orecchiette or bow-tie pasta

2 tablespoons extra-virgin olive oil

2 teaspoons fresh lemon juice

1 15-ounce can navy or cannellini beans, drained and rinsed

¾ to 1 pound hot-smoked salmon or smoked cod (haddock), flaked (see note)

¼ to ½ cup (or to taste) chopped Italian parsley or Italian spicy arugula

Freshly ground black pepper

Cook pasta in large quantity of boiling, lightly salted water according to package directions until just tender. Drain but do not rinse. Reserve. Whisk together olive oil and lemon juice. Combine pasta, beans, smoked fish, vinaigrette, and parsley or arugula. Serve in bowls with a few grinds of black pepper.

Note: if using smoked cod, poach the cod, covered, for 3 minutes in simmering mixture of equal parts water and milk; drain.

Beans and pasta provide textural contrast to each other, and a hearty background to smoked fish. Adding some extra freshly chopped parsley or arugula—if using cod—will further enliven both color and flavor.

Risotto with Peas and Smoked Salmon

Serves 4

successful risotto does require continuous attention after the cooking begins, but once the ingredients are prepared, completion of the dish requires relatively little time and the result is well worth the extra care. The basic technique lends itself well to including a variety of smoked seafood and meats as well, combined with crisp vegetables such as peas, snow peas, or scallions, or with chopped greens such as spinach or chard. The slight bitterness of some greens goes very well with the deeper smoky flavor that can suffuse the rice and sauce.

8 cups low-salt chicken or vegetable broth

¾ cup dry white wine

2 to 3 tablespoons extra-virgin olive oil

2 cloves garlic, minced

1 cup chopped onion

2 cups arborio rice

1 package frozen tiny peas, thawed (see note)

3 ounces freshly grated Parmesan cheese

6 to 8 ounces smoked salmon, diced (see note)

Heat broth and wine to simmer in pot. In a saucepan of at least 2-quart capacity, heat olive oil, add garlic and onion, and sauté briefly. Add rice to pot and stir until coated with oil. Add simmering broth slowly, about 1 cup at a time, stirring continuously over medium-high heat, until rice is almost tender and the sauce is almost creamy, about 20 to 25 minutes. Add the peas, then the Parmesan. Add the diced salmon just before serving, stirring gently to mix well. Serve immediately.

Note: An 8-ounce package of frozen, chopped spinach (thawed) can be added, either with the peas or in place of them. Smoked trout—2 fillets, about 4 ounces each, skinned and coarsely flaked—may be substituted for the smoked salmon.

Risotto with Smoked Mussels

Serves 4

8 to 9 cups low-sodium fish or chicken stock

1 tablespoon dried thyme or sage

3 tablespoons extra-virgin olive oil

1 cup chopped onion or scallions

1½ cups yellow or red bell pepper, chopped, or same amount of fresh or frozen, thawed peas

2 cups arborio rice

1 cup dry white wine or vermouth

10 to 12 ounces smoked mussel meats (preferably small)

Bring stock to simmer in a separate pot with thyme or sage. Heat olive oil in 4- to 6-quart nonstick pan. Add onion and sauté over medium heat until translucent. Add chopped bell pepper; cook 3 to 4 minutes. Add rice and wine to onion and pepper, turn up heat, and cook until liquid is almost gone. Reduce heat to medium-high and add simmering stock 1 cup at a time, stirring steadily. Continue until the rice is tender but firm. Add enough extra stock to make a slightly liquid sauce and stir in the mussels. Serve immediately.

While smoked shellfish are available canned in any supermarket, they can be mushy in texture and often lack the clarity of the smoky taste found in the freshly smoked variety. But if you find a brand of canned that suits your taste, it's definitely better than doing without. Both canned and freshly smoked shellfish are often packed in olive or vegetable oil, and this should be drained off—even rinsed off in the case of canned. No matter what type of freshly smoked shellfish is used, it is crucial that they be added at the end of the cooking process, with the last cup of liquid used, so that they are neither overcooked nor overly bludgeoned in the stirring this dish requires.

Orzo with Wild Rice and Smoked Fish or Shellfish

Serves 4

2 to 3 tablespoons extra-virgin olive oil

4 to 6 scallions, split lengthwise and chopped, with some of the green

1 cup orzo

2½ cups fish or chicken stock

2 to 3 ounces snow peas, in ½-inch slices, blanched, or peas, fresh or frozen, thawed

1 cup cooked wild rice

1 cup smoked mussels, bay scallops, flaked smoked haddock or cod, or hot-smoked salmon (see note)

½ cup chopped flat-leaf parsley

Risottos are especially welcome when made by someone else—someone who combines patience with tireless wrist action. Here are two more easily concocted variants made with the rice-shaped pasta called orzo. The addition of smoked fish (haddock, cod, salmon) and shellfish (mussels, scallops), perhaps with peas, asparagus, or greens, provides a medley of subtle creamy starch and stock studded with contrasting deep and bright flavors and a bit of crunch.

In a heavy-bottomed saucepan, heat olive oil over medium heat. Stir in scallions and cook until soft. Add the orzo and 1 cup of the stock; cover and cook over low heat until liquid is mostly absorbed, stirring occasionally to prevent sticking. Add additional stock gradually, about ½ cup at a time, stirring. When all the liquid has been just absorbed, stir in the snow peas, wild rice, and smoked fish or shellfish. Garnish with chopped flat-leaf parsley and serve.

Note: If using cold-smoked fish, poach fish in mixture of equal parts water and milk to cover for 2 to 3 minutes. Drain and flake.

Do-Ahead Risotto with Smoked Fish or Shellfish

Serves 4

¾ cup dry white wine (or dry vermouth, as Julia Child recommended)

1 cup arborio rice

1½ cups fish or chicken stock

½ cup asparagus or snow peas, in ½-inch pieces, or frozen peas, thawed

1 cup smoked mussel meats or bay scallops, or hot-smoked haddock, cod, salmon, or trout

½ cup chopped flat-leaf parsley

Freshly ground black pepper

In saucepan over medium heat, combine wine and rice; bring to a simmer and cook until wine is absorbed. Remove from heat. Allow to cool, then refrigerate. Shortly before serving time, add stock to rice and bring to a simmer, cooking until almost all the liquid is absorbed and rice is tender but still firm. Stir in vegetables and smoked seafood. Garnish each serving with parsley and some black pepper.

This technique was described by a guest chef in a *New York Times* column as one used in restaurants where constant stirring for half an hour is just not feasible.

Kedgeree

Serves 4

Kedgeree is a dish originally made up of bits of this and that—whatever was available. It usually combines traditional Scottish smoked haddock (finnan haddie) with curry powder seasoning and "sultanas," or golden raisins.

12 to 16 ounces smoked haddock, cod, or pollack, skinned, boned, and flaked

Milk as needed

1 medium onion, peeled, diced

1 tablespoon unsalted butter

1 cup long grain rice

1½ teaspoons curry powder

2 cups low-salt chicken stock, fish broth, or water

¼ cup golden raisins

Chopped parsley as needed

Poach fish in skillet with a mixture of equal parts milk and water to cover for 3 minutes. Remove fish to warm plate. Sauté onion in butter until liquid from onion evaporates, about 8 to 10 minutes. Add rice and curry powder, sauté briefly, then add broth or water. Bring to simmer and cook until liquid is absorbed. Stir in raisins. Mix flaked fish with rice, garnish with chopped parsley, and serve immediately.

Smoked-Haddock
(Finnan Haddie) Lasagna

Serves 6 to 8

2 to 3 leeks, sliced

2 tablespoons extra-virgin
olive oil

1 tablespoon butter

4 cloves garlic, minced or
pressed

1 pound mushrooms, sliced

Several grates of fresh
nutmeg

Kosher salt and freshly
ground black pepper

1 pound asparagus, tips only
(top third)

2 pounds smoked haddock
(finnan haddie)

3 to 4 cups milk (enough for
poaching the haddock)

18 sheets lasagna noodles

3 to 4 cups baby spinach
leaves

Freshly grated Parmesan
or Romano cheese

For the sauce

3 to 4 shallots, finely
chopped

6 tablespoons butter

7 tablespoons flour

1 cup half-and-half, warmed

1 cup milk, warmed

2 cups fish stock, warmed

½ cup dry white wine

1 tablespoon mustard

1 teaspoon smoked paprika
(see note)

1 teaspoon hot paprika

½ cup sherry

This is a dish to make for a crowd when you have time and are in the mood to do something a bit special. The results are well worth it, and this is real comfort food.

Recipe continued on next page ⟶

Smoked-Haddock (Finnan Haddie) Lasagna, continued

Sauté the leeks in the olive oil and butter until they soften. Add the garlic and sauté for 30 seconds. Remove leek mixture to bowl or plate; reserve. In the same pan, sauté the mushrooms until they are softened and lightly browned. Add several grates of fresh nutmeg and salt and pepper to taste about two-thirds of the way through cooking. Add the mushrooms to the leek mixture and stir to mix thoroughly. Steam the asparagus until just tender and reserve. Place the finnan haddie in a sauté or au gratin pan and pour in just enough milk to cover. (Or place in a mixture of equal parts milk and water.) Poach for about 5 minutes or until the flesh just starts to flake. Remove from liquid and skin, bone, and flake the fish. Reserve. Boil the lasagna noodles in a large quantity of lightly salted water and when done, drain and rinse with cold water.

While noodles cook, prepare the sauce. Sauté the shallots in the butter until softened. Add the flour and whisk for several minutes until the mixture starts to turn golden. Whisk in the warmed half-and-half and milk, stirring until well blended and smooth. Add the warm stock and the wine, whisking until the mixture is smooth. Bring to a boil, stirring constantly. Reduce heat to low and cook until thick, about 8 to 10 minutes, stirring occasionally. Season with the mustard and two paprikas and stir in the sherry. Remove from heat.

To assemble lasagna, preheat oven to 375°F. Rub the bottom of a 9 by 12 inch pan lightly with oil or butter. Spread a small amount of sauce in the bottom of the pan. Place a double layer of noodles on top of the sauce, then a single layer of spinach leaves, then one-third of the fish and one-third of the leek-mushroom mix. Add another thin layer of sauce, then repeat the noodles, spinach, fish, and leek-mushroom sequence two more times. Top the final layer with the asparagus tips, pour over the remaining sauce, and top with a generous layer of grated Parmesan or Romano. Bake for 15 to 20 minutes, until bubbling. Allow lasagna to sit for a few minutes to make cutting easier. Cut into squares and serve. Can be made a day ahead of time and simply reheated in the oven.

Note: Smoked paprika is available at specialty shops and online. See the Sources section, page 128.

Pizza with Chèvre and Smoked Salmon

Makes 4 appetizer portions

Pizza dough for one 12- to 14-inch pizza (see note)

Olive oil or vegetable oil as needed

Cornmeal as needed

1 cup soft chèvre (goat cheese), crumbled

1 cup julienned scallions (½ the green part
   included) or 1 cup julienned Chinese leeks

⅓-pound piece smoked salmon, sliced thinly
   into strips or julienned

½ cup coarsely chopped fresh basil, dill,
   oregano, or thyme (1 herb only)

Freshly ground black pepper

Lemon wedges as needed

The secret to using smoked salmon in making pizza is to think of it as the final topping, rather than as an ingredient that cooks along with the pizza. Fresh smoked salmon adds a silky texture and wonderful flavor to the goat cheese base. For even more flavor—Tricia's inspiration—spread onion marmalade over dough before goat cheese.

Preheat oven to highest temperature, 450°F to 500°F, 30 minutes before cooking. Ready the pizza topping ingredients while oven is heating. When the oven is ready—really hot!—prepare the pizza pan by oiling lightly with olive oil and dusting with cornmeal. Roll out the pizza dough on a floured board, transfer it to the pan, and press until it conforms to the shape of the pizza pan. Brush surface of the dough with olive oil and crumble half of the chèvre over it evenly. Scatter half of the scallions or leeks over the chèvre and place the pizza in the oven for about 15 minutes, or until the crust just begins to brown. Remove from the oven and cover surface evenly with the smoked salmon. Crumble the remaining chèvre over the top and sprinkle with the chopped herb of your choice and the remaining scallions or leeks. Anoint lightly with a drizzle of olive oil and sprinkle liberally with black pepper. Return to oven and bake no more than 3 to 4 additional minutes. The chèvre should just begin to melt and the crust should be a golden brown. (If you like a crispier crust, extend the initial baking for a few minutes. Don't let the salmon remain in the oven any longer than it takes the chèvre to soften.) Serve immediately with lemon wedges and more black pepper.

Note: Many supermarkets stock fresh pizza dough, usually in 1-pound lumps. For a thick crust, use the entire lump for this size pizza; or for a thinner crust, divide in half. (Refrigerated dough should be placed in a lightly oiled bowl, covered, and allowed to rise until at least double in size. This can require several hours from the time the dough is taken from the refrigerator. Then divide, knead briefly on a floured board, and let rest 10 minutes before rolling into shape.)

Potato-Poblano Lyonnaise with Smoked Fish

Serves 6 to 8

Julia Child, of course, pioneered in bringing the French gratin of potatoes to Americans' attention. This is a variation on those recipes and combines the mellow heat of roasted poblano peppers with the depth and warmth of smoked fish. Beautiful with a salad of crisp greens.

3 to 4 poblano peppers

3 cups thinly sliced onions

1 tablespoon butter

2 tablespoons extra-virgin olive oil, plus more as needed

5 to 6 russet potatoes, peeled and thinly sliced

Freshly ground black pepper

8 ounces smoked cod, haddock, or salmon, broken up into 1-inch flakes

2 cups grated Swiss cheese

2 to 3 cups chicken stock

Place the poblanos on foil under the broiler and turn periodically until the skins are blackened. (Alternately, if you have a gas range, place peppers on stove-top burner grates directly over medium-high flame, turning until blackened on all sides. Continue with the following directions.) Remove peppers from oven, place in paper bag, fold up the top of the bag, and let sit for 20 minutes. Remove peppers from bag, peel off the charred skin, seed, and slice into strips.

Preheat oven to 425°F. Sauté the onions in the butter and olive oil slowly over medium-low heat until lightly browned. Lightly coat the bottom of a 2- to 3-quart gratin pan with olive oil. Arrange a layer of potatoes on the bottom of the pan and season lightly with black pepper. Scatter a third of the onions and a third of the pepper strips across the potatoes and follow with a third of the flaked smoked fish and a third of the cheese. Continue with 2 more layers of potatoes, onions, peppers, smoked fish, and cheese so that the top layer is cheese. Pour in enough chicken broth to come up halfway inside the pan. Place in middle rack of oven and bake for 40 minutes. Test potatoes with fine skewer or paring knife for doneness. Remove from oven, let sit 10 minutes, and serve.

Peterson's Temptation

Serves 6 to 8

2 tablespoons vegetable oil

6 tablespoons softened butter

3 medium yellow onions, sliced (about 4 cups)

7 medium boiling potatoes (Yukon golds work very well) cut into ¼-inch by 3-inch batons (keep slices in cold water until dish is ready to be assembled)

8 ounces smoked whitefish, carefully checked for bones, flaked

Kosher salt and freshly ground black pepper

1½ cups heavy cream

⅓ cup dry bread crumbs

guest chef recipe

by Pete Peterson

Harlan "Pete" Peterson is the chef-owner of the renowned Tapawingo restaurant in Ellsworth, Michigan. This recipe is his take on the traditional Swedish potato dish called "Jansson's Temptation," which is usually made with anchovies. Instead of anchovies Pete substitutes smoked whitefish, a northern Michigan specialty.

Preheat oven to 400°F. Heat oil and 2 tablespoons butter in large skillet. When foam subsides add onions and cook about 10 minutes until onions just start to brown. Spread 1 tablespoon butter on bottom and sides of 2-quart casserole. Drain potatoes and dry with paper towels. Arrange a layer of potatoes on the bottom of the dish and then alternate layers of potatoes, onions, and whitefish, ending with potatoes. Sprinkle each layer with a little salt (depending on the saltiness of the smoked fish) and pepper. Heat cream in small pan until it comes to a simmer. Pour cream over potatoes. Mix bread crumbs and remaining softened butter together and spread over potatoes. Bake in center of oven 45 to 55 minutes or until potatoes are tender and cream is nearly absorbed. The bread crumbs should be golden brown. Check casserole midway, and if the crumbs are getting dark, loosely cover with sheet of aluminum foil to prevent further browning.

Recipe courtesy of Pete Peterson.

For St. Patrick's Day, the smokery offers simple smoked-salmon canapés on rounds of almost-crisp slices of boiled potato with chopped chive. The following recipes are a bit more elaborate but never obscure the natural affinity of smoked fish with earthy potato—another take on "surf and turf." Potato cakes in most forms are close cousins of the creamy or chunky brandades, light on the garlic and cream and nicely crusted for crisp and creamy contrast.

Sweet Potato Cakes with Smoked Cod

Makes 20 to 24 cakes

2 pounds sweet potatoes

2 pounds smoked cod or similar smoked fish

Milk as needed

1 large onion, finely diced

Freshly ground black pepper

Peanut or canola oil for frying

Flour as needed

Prick sweet potatoes all over with fork. Microwave on high for 12 to 15 minutes, turning once, or bake in 375°F oven for 1 hour. Let cool, cut in half lengthwise, and scoop out potato into large bowl, discarding peel. Mash with fork or put through a ricer or food mill. Poach smoked fish in equal parts milk and water to cover, about 5 minutes. Drain and flake into bowl with potatoes. Add onion and a grind or two of black pepper. Mix together lightly. Heat a very thin layer of oil in skillet until surface shimmers. Pat sweet potato mixture gently into cakes, dredge both sides lightly in flour, and sauté in oil until crisp and brown on each side. Drain briefly on paper towels on cooling rack. Serve immediately.

Serve as a side dish with Roasted Red-Pepper Sauce (see page 44), or as a main course with a salad.

Smoked-Cod Fritters

Makes about 20 fritters

2 pounds smoked cod or similar smoked fish such as haddock, catfish, or hake

Milk as needed

2 pounds russet potatoes, peeled and cut into approximately 1-inch cubes

1 medium onion, finely diced

6 cloves garlic, finely minced

½ cup chopped parsley

Yolks of 2 large eggs

1 tablespoon extra-virgin olive oil

Hot-pepper sauce to taste

Peanut or canola oil for frying

Poach smoked fish about 5 minutes in pan with equal parts milk and water to cover. Drain, cool, and flake into mixing bowl. Reserve. Cook potato chunks in lightly salted boiling water until tender, about 10 to 12 minutes. Rice potatoes or pass them through a food mill directly into mixing bowl. Add remaining ingredients except oil for frying. Gently fold mixture together. Form into balls about 1½ inches in diameter. Reserve.

In a Dutch oven or large heavy pot, heat about 3 inches of oil over medium heat until a dollop of batter crisps up immediately (about 350°F on a candy thermometer). Add fish balls in small batches to oil. When crisp and brown on the outside, remove to paper towels set on cooling rack to drain. Serve warm or at room temperature (you can rewarm slightly in a 250°F oven) before serving. Serve with hot-pepper sauce on the side.

Smoked-Cod Frittata

Serves 4 to 6

A dish inspired by the cooking of the Iberian Peninsula, with the cod or haddock standing in for salt cod. Eggs, potato, peppers, and onions—familiar enough. The smoked fish adds a background harmony to this combo, which is somehow both unusual and comfortingly familiar.

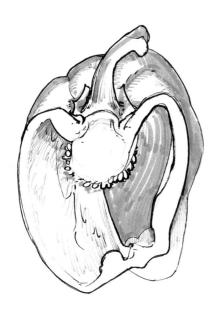

2 medium Yukon gold potatoes, peeled and cut into ½-inch cubes

½ to ¾ pound smoked cod or haddock

Milk as needed

6 large eggs

2 tablespoons heavy cream

Freshly ground black pepper

Light olive oil or vegetable oil as needed

½ each sweet red and green bell pepper, finely chopped

1 medium onion, finely chopped

Preheat oven to 400°F. Cook potato cubes in lightly salted water to cover. Simmer until tender, about 8 to 10 minutes. Drain and reserve. Poach fish in equal parts milk and water to cover, about 3 to 4 minutes. Drain, cool, and flake onto plate or into bowl. Lightly whisk together eggs, cream, and black pepper to taste. Reserve. Film a 10-inch cast-iron or ovenproof skillet with olive or vegetable oil over medium heat. Add bell peppers and sauté until soft. Add onion and sauté until translucent. Add reserved potato, stir, and sauté several more minutes. Add egg and cream mixture, stir in flaked smoked fish, and cook until eggs start to firm up but are still moist/runny. Transfer to oven and cook for 3 minutes. Remove and let sit at least 5 minutes before cutting into wedges.

Kuku with Smoked Trout

Serves 6 to 8

8 ounces smoked trout

4 tablespoons unsalted butter

1 medium onion, finely chopped

2 garlic cloves, minced

1 tablespoon flour

½ teaspoon baking soda

½ teaspoon salt, or less to taste

Freshly ground black pepper

1 tablespoon fresh lemon juice

5 large eggs

½ cup finely chopped mixed fresh herbs
(I like a combination of dill, cilantro, and parsley)

Preheat the oven to 350°F. Remove the skin from the smoked trout, then flake the fish. Reserve. In a medium skillet melt 2 tablespoons of the butter, then sauté the onion and garlic about 5 minutes, until just softened. Do not let them brown. Set aside. In a medium bowl mix together the flour, baking soda, salt, and pepper to taste. Stir in the lemon juice and mix well to remove any lumps, then immediately beat in the eggs. Place the remaining 2 tablespoons butter in a 9-inch pie plate. Set the plate in the preheated oven for a couple of minutes to melt the butter, being careful not to let it burn. Meanwhile, stir the flaked trout, the sautéed onion mixture, and the chopped herbs into the beaten eggs and mix well. Carefully remove the hot pie plate from the oven and pour the egg mixture over the melted butter. Return the plate to the oven and bake the omelet for 20 minutes, or until it is just set. Do not overbake. Serve hot or at room temperature.

Recipe courtesy of Darra Goldstein.

101

guest chef recipe

by Darra Goldstein

Darra Goldstein is the editor of *Gastronomica* and the author of several books, including *The Georgian Feast: The Vibrant Culture and Savory Food of the Republic of Georgia*. A *kuku* is a Persian-style omelet bursting with vegetables and herbs. Meat or fish is sometimes added, as in an Azerbaijani variation using local smoked whitefish. Here Goldstein substitutes smoked trout and bakes the omelet in the oven for a quick and foolproof dish that is truly delicious either for brunch or as a light supper with salad.

Smoked-Trout and Potato Salad with Chives

Serves 4

1 pound small new potatoes

2 tablespoons extra-virgin olive oil

1 tablespoon fresh lemon juice

½ cup chives, in 1-inch segments

1 teaspoon Dijon mustard

Several shakes hot-pepper sauce

Freshly ground black pepper

8 to 12 ounces smoked-trout fillet, skinned, coarsely chopped (see note)

Baby greens—romaine, arugula, assorted, sufficient to cover 4 salad plates

Bring potatoes to boil in lightly salted water to cover. Simmer 15 minutes or until tender. Drain and cool. Whisk together olive oil, lemon juice, chives, mustard, hot-pepper sauce, and black pepper to taste. Slice potatoes, place in serving bowl, add smoked trout, and toss with dressing. Serve over greens on salad plates.

Note: Use hot-smoked salmon or mackerel in place of trout. For these oilier fish, reduce olive oil to 1 tablespoon.

Smoked-Sablefish and Potato Salad

Serves 6 to 8

2 pounds medium Yukon gold potatoes

1 tablespoon fresh lemon juice

1 teaspoon extra-virgin olive oil

¼ cup capers, rinsed and drained twice,
   or same amount of caper berries, rinsed, drained,
   and coarsely chopped (see note)

½ medium red onion, very thinly sliced

1 pound smoked sable, sliced thinly
   (about ⅛ inch) (see note)

Flat-leaf parsley or Italian arugula leaves
   as needed

Bring potatoes to boil in lightly salted water to cover; reduce heat and simmer until tender, 20 to 30 minutes, depending on size. Drain, cool, and reserve. Whisk together the lemon juice, olive oil, and capers. Slice potatoes ¼ inch thick or slightly less; toss slices with dressing. Arrange potatoes on serving platter, scatter onion slices on top, array sablefish over all, and garnish with parsley or arugula.

Note: Substitute halved grape or cherry tomatoes for the capers/caper berries. For a variation on the smoked fish, this is another dish where smoked mackerel can do a good (and economical) stand-in.

The unctuous oil-richness of Alaskan sablefish, or Pacific black cod, is well set off by potato, sharp red onion, and capers or caper berries. The traditional "New York" sable-smoke is accomplished at a temperature somewhere between cold- and hot-smoking temperatures, and can be a bit saltier of necessity. The fish can still be sliced thin, even though it is heated during smoking just to the point where flaking begins but the oils are preserved. The richness of the sablefish calls for a sauvignon blanc with good acidity and citrus, or a more austere, minerally white such as a good Chablis.

Southwestern Black Bean and Corn Salad with Smoked Salmon or Cod

Serves 6 to 8

eans, sharing with potato a creamy-floury interior and earthy flavor, and corn, adding a crunchy sweet-starchiness with sunny color and flavor, singly and together work splendidly with a variety of smoked fishes. This dish is inspired by a black-bean tart with Southwestern seasonings that's always a crowd pleaser at our house, but it's a lot easier (no crust, for starters). Still very good though. This salad is fine with either hot-smoked salmon or smoked cod (haddock) that has been poached and flaked. With the red onion, sweet red pepper, corn kernels, and black beans, it's plenty colorful with either option. Though this looks like a salad to be served on the side, it's a terrific warm weather main dish as well.

1 to 1½ pounds hot-smoked salmon or smoked cod

Milk as needed

1 10-ounce package frozen corn kernels, thawed

1 15-ounce can black beans, drained and rinsed

1 sweet red bell pepper, cored, seeded, deveined, and chopped

1 medium red onion, chopped

½ cup chopped scallions

¼ cup pickled jalapeños, chopped (optional)

½ cup chopped cilantro (optional)

½ to ¾ cup quartered grape or cherry tomatoes (optional)

1 teaspoon each whole cumin and coriander seed (see note)

1 teaspoon chili powder, plus ½ teaspoon ground ancho chile if desired

3 tablespoons extra-virgin olive oil

2 tablespoons fresh lemon juice

Romaine leaves for each serving plate

Poach fish for 3 minutes in equal parts milk and water to cover. Drain, cool, and flake. Reserve. Spread corn kernels on greased baking sheet and toast in 300°F oven or in lightly oiled skillet over medium-low heat just until kernels begin to brown. Mix together corn, beans, bell pepper, onion, scallions, and, if desired, the jalapeños, cilantro, and tomatoes. Toast cumin and coriander seeds in dry pan over very low heat about 2 minutes until spices turn fragrant. Do not burn. Allow seeds to cool several minutes then grind in spice grinder. Whisk together ground cumin and coriander, chili powder, olive oil, and lemon juice. Toss flaked smoked fish with vegetables and dressing. Serve over romaine leaves.

Note: May substitute equal amounts very fresh ground cumin and coriander instead of toasting whole seeds.

Brandades

Smooth and Classic, New and Chunky

The classic French *brandade de morue,* a puree of salt cod (desalted by soaking in water and poaching in milk), garlic, potato, and cream, is a dream of a fish dish on its own. It is also a template for numerous variations using smoked white-fleshed fish such as cod, haddock, hake, or catfish instead of salt cod, and for dishes using oilier, fuller-flavored fish such as smoked mackerel, bluefish, or salmon. The potato-cream-garlic brandades are good fare for fall and winter; the chopped/mixed salad/spread versions are great warm weather treats, with the mix-ins adding a fresh look and crunch. White, black, broad, or fava beans, from scratch or canned, make a fine alternative to potato. Puree beans or mash partially for a chunky texture. Substitute the same volume or weight of beans for potatoes. Serve any of these brandades with sliced baguette or crackers—even in Belgian endive leaves.

With smoked cod or haddock this dish is actually easier to make than with salt cod—skip the 24-hour soak in at least 3 changes of water—and the smoking adds a nuanced flavor dividend as well. The curing and smoking process produces some of the texture and flavoring of the salted variety. Think of this as a dehydrated version of a hearty chowder, blended together for dipping or spreading. If you have a favorite garlic mashed potato recipe, simply flake the lightly poached smoked fish and fold in when adding the garlic cream to the mashed or riced potatoes.

Classic Smooth Brandade

Makes about 2½ cups

¼ cup good-quality extra-virgin olive oil

4 to 6 fresh sage leaves

1½ cups half-and-half

1 head garlic, cloves separated, peeled, and trimmed

1 pound to 1½ pounds russet potatoes, peeled, cut into 1½ inch pieces

1 pound smoked cod, haddock, pollack, or hake, skinned and boned

Simmer olive oil and sage leaves together in small pot for 20 minutes. Let cool. Remove sage leaves. In another small pan, simmer half-and-half with peeled garlic cloves for 20 minutes. Puree in blender; set aside to cool. Place potatoes in pot with water to cover, bring to boil, and simmer 12 to 15 minutes or until tender and easily penetrated with knife. Remove potatoes with scoop or pour into colander mounted over a second pot. Place pot with potato water on burner, place smoked fish in pot, and poach briefly, about 1 minute. Remove fish to plate and allow to cool. When cool, flake fish.

Warm garlic cream in microwave or in double boiler. Put potatoes through ricer or food mill. Add flaked smoked fish and gently fold in the garlic cream and infused olive oil to desired consistency. Serve immediately with toasted baguette slices or crackers.

Semismooth Brandade

Makes about 3 cups

1 pound smoked cod, haddock, pollack, or hake, skinned and boned

2 pounds russet potatoes, unpeeled

1 whole head of garlic

Bring enough water to cover fish to a simmer in a saucepan. Place fish in water and poach briefly, about 1 minute. Remove fish, drain, and allow to cool. When fish is cool, flake and reserve. Rub potatoes with olive or vegetable oil and sprinkle with salt. Pierce potatoes lightly here and there with the tip of a knife. Slice about a half inch off the blossom end of the garlic head to expose the cloves and brush cut side with olive or vegetable oil. Put garlic cut side up, along with potatoes, in a large roasting pan and bake in a 350°F oven about 1 hour and 15 minutes, or until potatoes are easily penetrated with a skewer or knife. Cut potatoes in half lengthwise and scoop out baked potato. Squeeze out the baked garlic cloves into the potatoes (they'll slip from their skins easily) and mix potatoes and garlic together lightly. Add flaked fish, mixing everything together gently with a fork. Serve in communal terrine or gratin with toasted baguette slices.

This easy-to-prepare brandade expands the concept by incorporating diced boiled or roasted potato instead of mashed or pureed. In place of cream, a light olive oil dressing provides a moist binding medium. And rather than reaching its flavor and texture potential through pureeing and blending, it relies on a mixture of chopped or minced ingredients to better exploit their complementarities by maintaining the contrasts in flavor and texture. A sprinkling with either Hungarian sweet or Spanish smoked paprika goes well with either the tapas or the hash and eggs versions. A light dusting with curry powder goes nicely with the mackerel or bluefish.

Chunky "Skillet Hash de Brandade" with Smoked Fish

Serves 6 to 8

Extra-virgin olive oil as needed

½ cup diced onion

2 cloves garlic, minced

½ cup diced sweet red bell pepper, or ½ cup cherry or grape tomatoes, pulp removed

1½ pounds cooked redskin or fingerling potatoes, large dice

1 to 1½ pounds smoked fish (see note)

¼ cup capers, well rinsed

Chopped parsley (optional)

Film skillet with olive oil over low to medium heat. Add onion, garlic, and bell pepper or tomato and sauté 5 minutes. Add potatoes and sauté until warmed through. Flake smoked fish and mix into skillet. Stir in capers. Add about a tablespoon of olive oil. If you wish, add chopped parsley just before serving.

Serve warm or let come to room temperature. This can be served as a tapas-style spread. Also excellent as a savory hash with poached or fried egg on top.

Note: If using cold-smoked fish, poach fish in equal parts milk and water 3 to 5 minutes. Drain and reserve. If using hot-smoked salmon, trout, bluefish, or mackerel, reduce the amount of fish by about one-third, especially for the more strongly flavored bluefish or mackerel. No need to poach the fish.

A Primer on Do-It-Yourself Smoking

Taking the Cure: Wet Bath, Dry Bath, or Rubdown and Relax

If you're an avid reader of food news, gourmet magazines, or restaurant reviews, in the past few years you've undoubtedly noticed a veritable barrage of items on brining meats—usually poultry or pork—prior to cooking. Brining, or soaking in a salt-and-water solution, often seasoned with herbs, spices, fruit juices, or wine, for hours or days, is touted as enhancing the flavor, moisture, and texture of meats that otherwise are considered rather bland or that tend to dry out during cooking.

If you've gone on to try this at home, you've encountered the first essential stage—and some of its virtues—in the curing and smoking process: infusing the stuff to be smoked with salt and giving the salt enough time to work a transfiguration of the proteins in the meat or fish. You can actually tell the difference between the fresh and the brined before cooking—brined meat has a springier, more resilient feel, a livelier elasticity than the fresh. Once you have roasted a piece of meat you have brined, you know why it is a technique in traditional French charcuterie (see Jane Grigson's excellent discussion of "salt pork and ham" in her *The Art of Charcuterie*).

Brining is one of three basic methods for salting fish or meat at the initial stage of curing and smoking. It lends itself to either cold- or hot-smoking and is an efficient means of using large chunks of salt—which was important when grinding salt was difficult and costly. Its main advantage these days is that it provides predictable, uniform salt concentrations in the meat or fish in a relatively short time.

Today, salt is available from coarse to very fine grinds or crystals, which makes possible two alternative ways to apply salt prior to smoking. One is simply to bury meat or fish in very coarse salt, giving it a dry-salt "bath," which draws out moisture while some salt dissolves and is absorbed by the flesh. The second method is to rub or dredge salt onto the flesh and then allow sufficient time for it to be absorbed. Seasonings may be combined with the salt, as is done in Scandinavia to make the classic gravlax, salmon cured with salt, sugar, spices, and fresh dill. Either approach works well for cold-smoking. Unlike brining, these two methods can be used only with fresh, not previously frozen, ingredients, and each requires a more customized approach for each type and cut of meat or fish.

Smoking Cold or Hot: The "Raw" or the "Cooked"

While salting and drying play important parts in making smoked meats and fish, the smoke itself—obviously—plays a significant role as well. Smoke is composed of hundreds of chemicals. Some of these add preservative value, while others contribute to flavor. Smoke seems to forestall oxidation of fats and oils—an important activity, since many of the fish and meats that produce superior smoked products are relatively high in fats or oils—salmon and mackerel, bacon and ham.

Today most smoked foods are designated as hot- or cold-smoked, though there are in fact many variations in times and temperatures within these categories. For some products, a period of cold-smoking may precede a final hot-smoking. But for both meats and fish, the final results of cold- and hot-smoking are sufficiently different to warrant an easy divide, separated by a "no-smoking zone" between 90°F and 110°F.

Of the two, cold-smoking is the most direct continuation of the curing process that begins with salting. Cold-smoking can follow any of the salting methods, though it may seem intuitively to have a more natural affinity with the dry-salting methods. Indeed, the primary objective of cold-smoking is to sustain the drying process. In doing so, cold-smoking results in less perishable foods than does hot-smoking, largely by promoting drying and, to a lesser extent, by adding to the air flow small amounts of chemical compounds that aid preservation or provide a protective coating against insects or oxygen.

It may be called cold-smoking, but a lot of it occurs at comfortable room temperatures, though it can be done slightly warmer and significantly colder. The essential trick to cold-smoking is to keep the temperature low enough, while drawing smoke from a (hot) fire or smolder. Temperatures between 90°F and 110°F promote bacterial growth, and at temperatures above 110°F proteins begin to "cook," hardening the surface and interfering with the drying process. Thus cold-smoking/drying is done below 90°F, often between 70°F and 90°F for a period of 12 to 72 hours. In some areas, such as Alaska, smoking may be done below 40°F over a period of weeks.

Hot-smoking, on the other hand, is less a means of preservation than it is a way of cooking that imparts a smoky flavor. The brining or salt bath may affect the texture and the shelf life of the finished product, if given adequate time to do its transformative work. The smoking, usually at relatively low cooking temperatures in the 160°F to 190°F range, works in conjunction with the brine cure on the final flavor and texture but effectively brings the curing process to a halt, in contrast to cold-smoking. The higher salt content of hot-smoked products extends their keeping qualities beyond fresh or fresh cooked, but not to the extent achieved by the salting and drying combined in cold-smoking.

When done properly, the brining cure prior to hot-smoking works a metamorphosis in the texture and moisture of the meat, which again will largely determine the quality of what comes out of the hot-smoking. Following brining, the meat or fish must be air-dried, or given a cold-smoking, until a "pellicle" or salt glaze covers the surface. (See the "Smoke and Errors" section later in this chapter for more details on this.) Without the pellicle, the further loss of moisture, fats, or oils during the cooking phase will result in a drier, tougher finished product.

Hot-smoking is similar to barbecue (well, some kinds of barbecue—that's another subject entirely!). Barbecue—real barbecue, not grilling—takes time. Hot-smoking takes time twice—once for the salt curing and once for the smoking or smoke roasting. It's the salt-curing time and ingredients that make the difference. And since time is money, it's the curing time that is the first to go in commercial smokehouses. Which may be the reason so many establishments refer to a smokemaster rather than to a curemaster, who has been replaced with brine tanks or brine injector needles.

Where There's Smoke, There's—
Logs, Chunks, Chips, Dust

Every region has its smoke of choice, and everyone from backyard smokers to the smokemasters of prestige producers swears by one wood or another, or a secret blend. Equally strong opinions range widely on the subject of what form of wood should be used—whole logs, wood chips, sawdust.

Oak has long been associated with Scottish and Irish smoked salmon, but beech has a European following as well, and juniper is added to the mix in Scandinavian countries. Alder is the swear-by, full-flavor staple of the Pacific Northwest for salmon and other fish or game. And hickory is the mainstay of the American Midwest and South—usually for hot-smoking meats or poultry. Applewood, pecan wood, cherry, pear—all have their advocates, either on their own or in blends with hardwoods, applewood often being used to smoke pork. Maple is common in the northern Midwest, and corncobs are popular in parts of New England. In central and northern Europe juniper and cedar have a following and once provided the dark resinous preservative husk on hams from those regions. Grapevine cuttings in parts of California and France give a mild, sweet smoke. The current mystique of mesquite, a hot-burning wood popular in restaurant and backyard grilling, does not extend to cold-smoking.

Hot-smokers, needing higher temperatures and seeking the spiciness from wood fires, may favor logs and chunks, but cold-smokers rely more on chips and sawdust, keeping the smoldering well removed from the items to be smoked. Peat, which only smolders, is used in parts of Ireland, Scotland, and the Shetlands, though not in commercial smokehouses. In other parts of the world, availability dictates what fuels might be relied upon, and not all of these will come directly (and unprocessed) from the field or forest.

Hot or Cold: Fish, Fowl, or the Other White Meat?

With the exception of the European or "nova lox" versions of smoked salmon, and occasionally sturgeon, the most familiar smoked fish are hot-smoked, as travelers in search of local gustatory delights along our coasts know full well:

bluefish on the American East Coast, Pacific salmon on the West Coast, mackerel on the East Coast from Maine to Florida, sable or black cod in Alaska or Brooklyn, whitefish or chubs along the Great Lakes, catfish in the American South, mullet and amberjack on the Gulf coast, and trout almost everywhere.

Two well-known exceptions are kippered herring and finnan haddie (haddock), both brined and cold-smoked but intended to be cooked before eating. In fact, most of these fishes can be cold-smoked, but they must be supremely fresh and in fine condition. While the end result can be a delicacy, it is one that many people, at least in the United States, approach with some hesitation. For example, I've had cold-smoked catfish that in flavor and texture rivaled the best offerings of New York City delis, but I suspect it will be a cold July in Mississippi before it pushes salmon or sable aside in popularity. Bluefish and mackerel, if very fresh and dry-cured in the manner of gravlax, make a cold-smoked delicacy but one somewhat contrary to American experience and expectations.

In Europe cold-smoked or air-cured game, fowl, and ham are regional specialties encountered or even eagerly sought after by travelers. But in the United States when it comes to poultry or pork by far the most familiar versions are hot-smoked—chicken, turkey, fresh pork leg, pork loin or chops, duck, pheasant. All of these are fair game for the avid backyard smoker.

Cold-smoking promotes a subtle melding of smoke and other flavors and a pliable, resilient texture in both meat and fish. A definite "smokiness" can be elusive, even though the use of different woods will impart noticeable differences in the finished product. In many renditions, the fish or meat is so transformed from its original state that it may be difficult to associate it with the original fresh ingredient, except by similar shape and size. Hams or salmon can be sliced paper thin into almost translucent pieces that can be draped, wrapped, or furled in various presentations. Hot-smoked fish are flakier in texture and cannot be thinly sliced. Usually, they are smokier as well, and can be accompanied with more assertive condiments such as mustard or even horseradish sauce. Hot-smoked meats or poultry are more closely comparable to the fresh-cooked version, but usually with a denser, firmer texture due to the cure they take on during the brining.

Smoke and Errors: Basic Recipe with Equipment, Ingredients, Suggestions for the Backyard

Since the technical requirements for successful and safe cold-smoking are either too stringent or expensive for backyard experimentation (regardless of what some equipment manufacturers may tell you or some books on the subject may suggest), this section will focus solely on hot-smoking. When I first began smoking salmon, I felt that cold-smoking was the only way to go, affording the greatest range for experimenting with seasonings and subtle variations in curing and smoking. Perhaps this was due to a Midwestern upbringing overexposed to bacon, ham, and hickory smoke. Now, I'm finding that hot-smoking with brined meats or fish offers a much wider range of experimenting and culinary discovery than I had at first imagined. The trick I think is first to develop a central process or technique and then to work variations on it with seasonings, ingredients, and smoke. Each new effort will require some experiment, but homing in on something new and really good will take only a few trials. Fortunately, most errors remain enjoyably edible.

Equipment: For consistent temperature, electric smokers are the most predictable. Luhr Jensen makes an economical aluminum box smoker in two sizes, with heating elements adapted to each size. Brinkmann and Weber make electric silo-shaped smokers that can be used for barbecue as well and come with water pans. Weber charcoal kettles and Oklahoma/Texas barrel smokers with separate fireboxes can be used as well.

Ingredients: A general purpose basic brine recipe will work for fish such as salmon or bluefish fillets cut into uniformly sized pieces, trout or mackerel fillets, turkey breast, or pork loin. For larger pieces such as whole turkey breast or chunks of pork loin, brining times should be increased to 4 or 5 days. Experiment with different seasonings. Ingredients such as soy sauce, ginger, garlic, onion, thyme, juniper, allspice, bay, star anise, apple juice or cider, cranberry juice, molasses, or maple syrup can turn your smoker into a culinary laboratory.

Salt: Kosher (uniodized) salt is best. I prefer Kosher Diamond Crystal, and the volume-based recipe assumes this brand. Diamond brand pickling salt is chemically the same but is cut much finer (use one-quarter less by volume). For sugars/sweeteners, I like turbinado, or raw, sugar, which is good for flavor and color. Domino "Brownulated" light brown works well, as does Sucanat (a brand of unrefined cane sugar). For most of these, the crystal size works well for the volume-based recipe here. If you use a standard white granulated sugar, you may want to add some unsulfured molasses for flavor, but it's not necessary.

You will need 1 gallon of brine for each 3 pounds of fish or meat, cut in uniform sizes. Because the brine concentration is low, the pieces will not float, but will stay submerged, which is good. For salmon, cut 3-pound boneless fillets crosswise at 2-inch intervals. Brine salmon under refrigeration in a tightly covered container for 48 hours, stirring at least twice over this period using a clean spatula or spoon each time. For boneless pork loin, cut into chunks 4 to 6 inches long; for turkey breast, separate the whole breast into the 2 lobes. Brine pork or turkey chunks for at least 3 full days, and up to 5, stirring once a day.

Mix salt and sugar, 3 cups to 1 cup. Use 1 cup of this mixture per gallon of water. If you are using seasonings other than soy sauce (Lite Soy from Kikkoman is good, at 1/4 to 1/2 cup per gallon of brine), simmer them briefly with 1 cup of the salt/sugar mix in a quart or so of water before adding to the brine (count this cup of salt/sugar in the total number to be combined with water). Use a deep, food grade bucket—available at restaurant supply stores, usually in a calibrated 5-gallon size.

Suggested seasonings: granulated garlic and/or onion with soy sauce, possibly with powdered ginger (about ½ tablespoon each per gallon); allspice with coriander and black pepper (1 tablespoon each whole, simmered with part of brine, per gallon); juniper berries with bay leaf (6 berries, 3 leaves per gallon, simmered); apple cider or juice with allspice, 1 cup per gallon. Other "additives" to experiment with are unsulfured molasses, maple syrup, cranberry juice, and star anise with ginger and soy sauce. And don't forget standby herbs like thyme, fennel, sage, and rosemary—they are standbys for good reason. It's a good idea to keep the combinations simple, say, 2 or 3 items, to get a good idea of how they work with different fish or meats and to avoid muddying the flavors.

This next step is critical, and you skip it at your peril. When brining is completed, blot pieces dry with paper towels (salmon will feel much firmer, more resistant to pressure than fresh). Lay pieces, uncovered, on wire racks placed over cookie-sheet pans in refrigerator overnight to dry. Or air dry with a fan for several hours at a temperature below 70°F. When the meat or fish is sufficiently dry, a salt glaze or "pellicle" will have formed over the surface, which will be slightly tacky to the touch. This pellicle protects against further drying and helps in developing a good depth of smoky flavor. Now you're ready to smoke. (If you wish to dust the flesh with spices or herbs, do it just before starting the drying process so that the seasoning is embedded in the pellicle.)

Place pieces in the smoker, fill the smoking chip pan, and turn on the heat. Ideally, you are shooting for a peak sustained temperature in the 170°F to 180°F range—this is where experimenting with your particular smoker comes in, with an eye on the outside temperature as well. You will find that internal smoker temperatures vary considerably from bottom (hotter) to top (cooler, even though heat rises) too. You can compensate for this by putting thinner, smaller pieces on top racks. The internal temperature of the meat or fish should reach 145°F and be held there for at least 30 minutes. (Inexpensive digital thermometers with cable probes are now available at kitchen and restaurant supply stores.)

Depending on your smoker's operating temperature, the outside temperature, the amount of meat or fish you are smoking, and the kind of wood chips used, plan on 2 or 3 hours of smoking time, at a minimum. Some smokers, such as the Luhr Jensen, can take a bit longer—check the manufacturer's manual or operating guidelines. Barrel-type smokers with offset firebox and fired with a load of charcoal smothered in damp sawdust, or with burning wood chunks, will easily reach 200°F to 250°F, especially in summer temperatures.

If you are doing larger pieces such as whole bone-in or boneless turkey breast or pork loin chunks and find that your smoker runs at the lower end of the temperature range, you may want to finish the cooking in a very slow (200°F) oven, under a loose foil wrap, for an additional 2 to 3 hours or until they feel quite firm to a finger poke or the temperature probe reads 155°F for at least 30 minutes.

Meats or fish brined and hot-smoked in this way have a longer shelf life than freshly cooked. Wrap in plastic and keep refrigerated for up to 10 days. Or wrap and freeze. If frozen, thaw in the refrigerator overnight.

Serving: Fish such as salmon will be flaky in texture. Pieces may be cut up with a sharp knife, flaked onto salad greens, or chopped and mixed with onion and sweet pepper or celery for a salad or spread. Smaller pieces, or those that get overcooked and possibly a bit dried out, can be combined with cream cheese or sour cream with herbs for spreads or dips. Meats can be thinly sliced and are best served this way. They are nicely accompanied with sharp mustards or a nippy horseradish sauce, and work well in sandwiches and in salad presentations.

Smoky Roasting with Your Charcoal Kettle: A Simple, Sure-Fire, Tried and True Method for Great Results

This section answers one burning question: How can I roast large hunks of meat, fish, or poultry on my charcoal kettle grill and get that great smoky flavoring time after time without too much fuss, bother, and generally screwing up? Put another way, how can my charcoal kettle realize its destiny and fulfill its existential potentiality in my own backyard, without my own fear and trembling? Easy. Just make sure you have some essential equipment.

Weber charcoal kettle grill (or similar model), 22 ½-inch size: The "One-Touch"

Weber offers better ventilation than the basic model (but it's not necessary to have the more expensive "Master-Touch" with ash catcher and thermometer).

Useful Weber Optional Equipment: "V"-shaped roast rack and the Weber rib rack are both quite useful for best positioning of meats or ribs and for an easily removed and cleaned rack. A hinged grill grate, also available from Weber, is very helpful for adding charcoal and/or smoking chips more easily for extended time smoky roasting. None of these is essential for consistently good results.

Fire Starter Chimney: An easy way to start your charcoal fire without starter fluids; also helps measure amount of briquettes to be used for most recipes. With 2 full sheets of crumpled newspaper and one good kitchen match, you can get reliable start-up in 15 to 20 minutes, and your grill won't look or smell like a backyard incinerator for toxic wastes. Weber now offers an oversized starter chimney, with briquette capacity sufficient even for those who feel a bed of charcoal should look like a major lava flow. (If you think you just must have more than the chimney can accommodate, or want to assure a longer-burning bed of coals, put extra briquettes around the chimney and dump the ignited contents on top, then stir and spread with a poker or other suitable instrument.)

Water Pan: Deep disposable aluminum baking pans or similar available from Weber. May use a regular metal baking pan (9 inch by 12 inch) lined with heavy-duty aluminum foil for easier cleanup. A water pan is most useful where much fat is rendered during the cooking process, as with duck or pork shoulder. It provides a good place for the fat to go, without flare-ups, and makes the cleanup bearable. Also good in some slow-cooking recipes to maintain moistness and keep the burning coals off the side instead of directly under the meat.

Charcoal Briquettes: I recommend Kingsford for easy starting and consistent, predictable burning. You may want to experiment with hardwood charcoals or other briquettes, but expect to take a try or two before you are confident of the results.

Fire Shovel or Poker: For spreading burning briquettes or mixing in new briquettes.

Pam nonstick pan spray or vegetable oil applied with paper towels.

Fish Grill Grids or Fish Grill Basket: Removable, washable grids, 12 inches square or so, can make cleanups easier if sprayed with Pam before use, and they are very useful if you are grilling or smoking vegetables such as onions, eggplants, tomatoes, etc. A fish grill basket can be useful for easier handling of whole fish or larger portions thereof if you wish to turn the fish during cooking. It's just as easy to put a second fish grill on the top and turn the whole assembly over (wearing fireplace gloves!), and the grills are more versatile. Spray with Pam before use for less sticking and much easier cleanup. The perforated, porcelain-coated models are most versatile—excellent for vegetables as well—and easiest to clean. If the grill grid is well oiled, it is possible to flip fish fillets with a spatula or spatula-tongs implement. If you do a lot of fish, it's worth it to get the special elongated fish-spatula model.

Heavy Gloves/Tongs: For lifting hot grill to add charcoal or for lifting hinged sections of grill for same purpose.

Smoking Chips (with steel or aluminum bowl for soaking): For consistent and clean flavors and predictable performance, I prefer those from Luhr Jensen, which come in a variety of "flavors." Try alder, apple, cherry, and perhaps hickory blended with lighter fuels such as apple. Avoid mesquite! Other chips available on the market are fine as well, but be sure they are adequately soaked in water before adding to charcoal—several hours at least to be on the safe side. Chips can be soaked in apple juice or cider, rum, bourbon, or sherry for additional flavoring. For soaking, a 1-quart stainless steel mixing bowl such as Farberware is ideal.

Assorted Herbs and Spices, Black Pepper, and Kosher Salt: For composing sprinkles, rubs, pastes, marinades. Garlic and onion powder, paprika, thyme and sage, lemon juice, and olive oil are the basics. Juniper berries, allspice, cumin, clove, and cinnamon lend interesting flavor notes. Juniper berries, allspice, and bay leaf can be added to the chips for extra herbal zip to the smoking.

Warning: *Do not* attempt with a gas grill; it won't work, and you'll only end up feeling a bit silly. Gas-fired grills *are* convenient for spur-of-the-moment grilling fits—but they are grills, not roasting kettles, and they are not vented to permit a steady flow of freshly generated smoke to flow around the meat.

Basic Technique: Advance Preparation

At least 1 hour before actual cooking time fill a 1-quart mixing bowl about three-quarters full of selected smoking chips. Add water to the brim, and soak until cooking time. Larger chips and chunks should soak at least 2 hours before adding to coals. (Before soaking, pick out any bark—this can impart a noticeable and undesirable bitterness to the smoke.)

Twenty minutes before cooking time: Crumple 2 full sheets (double page) of newspaper and stuff into bottom end of fire chimney. With fire chimney resting on bottom grate of kettle, fill with charcoal briquettes (depending on what you are cooking, this is a time to scatter additional briquettes on the bottom of the grate for longer fire life, but they can be added later as well). Light the newspaper in several spots around the base of the chimney. After about 20 minutes most of the briquettes in the chimney should be glowing, at least around the edges.

Just before replacing top grill grate and placing meat on for roasting, dump burning briquettes onto bottom grate and mix with additional briquettes (if called for in the recipe). Whether coals are spread evenly over the grate, or pulled to one side, or placed on both sides of a water-filled drip pan depends on what's being roasted. If a water pan is used, it should be moved into position—center, or on one side—just before emptying the charcoal onto the grate. Allow 10 minutes or so for the new briquettes to ignite. Squeeze out (with small chips or coarse sawdust) or shake off excess water and scatter smoking chips over the charcoal. Use handful clumps with small chips to maximize smoking time.

To start smoke-roasting: Replace the top grill grate on the kettle, position meat or fowl on grate as recipe indicates, and place kettle lid firmly over the kettle so that most of the smoke escapes through the open lid damper holes.

Then either wait until total cooking time has elapsed or until it's time to add additional charcoal and/or smoking chips. When meat is done, it's best to remove from the heat and let it sit for 15 to 20 minutes before serving.

That's all there is to it!

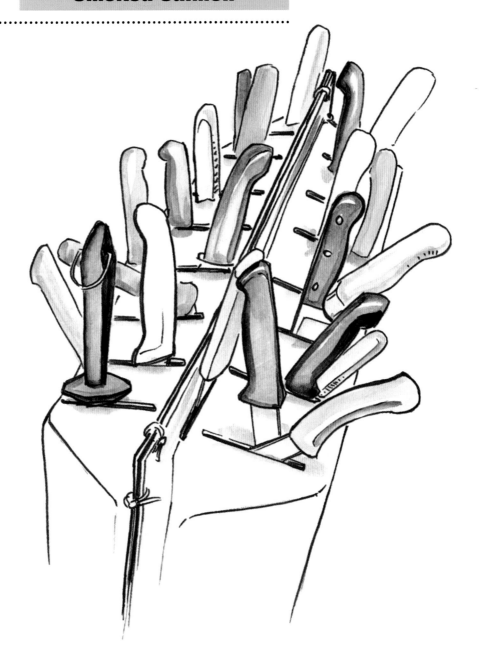

Smoked salmon is widely available sliced and vacuum packed in supermarkets and at specialty food or fish retailers. Hand-sliced smoked salmon has of course been a centerpiece of the deli, where the expertise of counter staff slicing large, transparently thin pieces from whole sides is a compelling show. How much of this performance is due to marketing, of a once quite expensive, and often quite salty, luxury food, we'll leave to others. Suffice it to say, large, thin pieces make for a generous display of what is, by weight, very little.

From the beginning, Tracklements has concentrated on selling smoked salmon by the piece, emphasizing freshness and versatility over convenience. Of course, this leaves the slicing to the customer. While initially daunting to many, the challenge is easily overcome with a serviceable knife, a bit of stick-to-it-iveness, and very little practice. And there's the added advantage, even, one could say, convenience, of being able to render slices or other cuts more appropriate to particular uses or presentations than are afforded by the one-slice-fits-all smoked-salmon packages.

First, the knife. It need not be the special, expensive, 12-inch salmon slicer featured in cookware catalogs. A thin, fairly long (10 inches) blade, moderately flexible and well sharpened, works quite well. A good choice is the Granton 10-inch all purpose slicer, useful for most meats as well as salmon. It's recommended by *Cook's Illustrated* and available at KnifeMerchant.com, at a very good price, with prompt, excellent service. A 9- to 10-inch fillet knife, such as Chicago Cutlery or Dexter-Russell, is quite serviceable.

Butchering is not, in our common usage, heavy with connotations of craft or artfulness. However, it is one way to approach a whole side of cold-smoked salmon. Hot-smoking salmon and other fish renders all parts pretty much the same in terms of flakiness, and makes a fork more useful for serving than a knife. There are roughly three situations to be dealt with in moving from cutting board to serving platter: the whole side; dividing the side into "primal cuts," each offering somewhat different advantages and requiring somewhat different approaches; and slicing, preparing for presentation, combining with other ingredients, and consumption.

Confronting first a whole side of cold-smoked Atlantic salmon, preferably trimmed of belly and 3 to 4 inches off the tail end, position the side so that as a right- or left-hander, you are able easily to slice toward the tail end. For a right-hander, the tail end would be to the right, and slicing would be moving from left to right toward the tail. For approximately 2-inch slices, each the width of the salmon fillet, lay the knife almost flat against the surface, 2 inches or so from the end. With light pressure, ease the edge of the knife just under the surface and, keeping the blade almost horizontal, slice gently and smoothly—you'll know what this means after a couple whacks—toward the tail. Continue slicing, starting at the left edge of the sliced surface, and working slightly downward at a very shallow angle, continue making additional slices, removing from the skin at the end of the slice. Continue working back toward the head, or "collar," end of the salmon. You should be able to get at least 60 thin slices from the side, which can run 2½ to 3½ pounds after trimming.

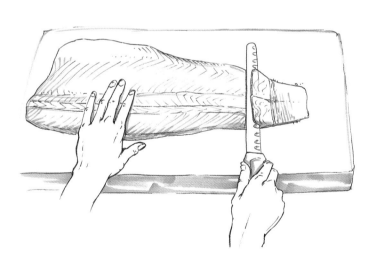

Some finer points. You will notice as you move along the salmon fillet that the central part of each slice will have a darker wedge-shaped portion in the lower middle. This is perfectly edible, but you may wish to remove it for aesthetic reasons. It can be cut out as a triangular piece, or, if you wish to serve pieces smaller than the full, fillet-wide slice, it can be removed by dividing each slice into 2 or 3 pieces in such a way that the dark triangle remains on the cutting board.

Now the "primal cuts." At the smokery we customarily package salmon sides into three or four pieces: a "collar cut," about 6 inches down the fillet from the head end; the "center cut," the next 6 inches or so; and a "tail cut" of 6 to 9 inches. Often we divide the "center cut" lengthwise down the middle into a belly cut (smoother, homogeneous consistency, with more oil) and a back-loin cut. These make nice ½-pound pieces, whereas the others are usually ⅔ to ¾ pound and the tail cuts run up to 1⅓ pounds.

Which cut do you want, and why? If you want slices of relatively firm and even texture, somewhat lighter in flavor, the tail cut is the thing. You can start at the wider end of this piece (closer to the head), with the tail end off to your left (for right-handers), and get fairly wide slices of even consistency, working back to the tail end. I know, this seems to contradict the instructions for a whole side, but bear with me. If you have a whole side, you can separate the tail cut from the other two-thirds toward the head, and slice the tail cut as described here, and then do the remaining side (collar cut plus center cut) as above, slicing toward the tail end. Why? Read on.

If you are dealing with either the collar cut, the center cut, or the two together as just described, you want to slice toward the tail end. This is because, for the Atlantic salmon and reasons best left to Poseidon, if you slice the other way the slices tend to unfurl into less manageable forms. Actually, this section of the fillet is composed of the back-loin—several muscle groups sandwiched together—and the belly, a more homogeneous, velvety piece. These cuts, including the one piece or the other of the divided center cut, are equally well suited for any uses requiring thin slices, as well as for thicker "sushi" slices or larger pieces for sautéing or grilling.

When dealing with the collar or center cuts, how can you tell which end is closest to the tail, since the tail end is not there? Poseidon has provided telltale clues—along the back-loin, a series of chevron or arrow-type markings point toward the tail end (there are similar chevron markings on the belly, but these may have been completely or partially trimmed off). Start at the end the chevrons point to and work back up toward the head end.

Sources of Smoked Salmon and Other Seafood

In the world of cured and smoked seafood, as in other culinary realms, there are those who make, and those who sell—the producers and the purveyors. Some producers sell direct as well, either through their local retail outlet, through mail order, or both. I'll focus on the producers here, with some reference to selected retail outlets for some of these.

In the United States, the smoked-fish/seafood scene has undergone substantial evolution over the past thirty years. In the past, with the exception of a few large New York City smokehouses (Marshall's, Acme) and smaller places along the East and West Coasts, most of the high-end smoked salmon was imported from Canada, Scotland, England, Ireland, Norway, even Switzerland. In the mid-1970s, Des Fitzgerald started **Ducktrap of Maine** (www.ducktrap.com), producing a wide range of smoked fish and shellfish, from salmon and trout to monkfish and mussels. Around the same time, Homarus set up small-scale smoking operations on the edge of New York City, beginning with trout. The last fifteen years or so have seen more developments in the domestic smoked-seafood scene, from mergers among the large producers to start-up boutique smokers, with innovative approaches well beyond the traditionally charted smoked-fish waters.

Today, Ducktrap is basically a brand name owned by a large seafood company; while at least some of their smoked-salmon products come from Maine, other fish such as mackerel are smoked for them in the Shetlands. Their products are distributed nationally through supermarket chains and specialty food stores. Once an independent mail order source, Ducktrap now appears in various mail order catalogs, such as Mackenzie. Over the past fifteen years, it has been joined on the East Coast by a number of new smoked-fish companies, several of which have national distribution as well. **Spence & Co. Ltd.** (www.spenceltd.com) emphasizes the Scottish lineage of Michael Spence. This company produces an array of smoked fish, from salmon and haddock (finnan haddie) to mackerel, and a number of ready-to-serve canapé preparations. In the late 1990s, **Stonington Sea Products** (www.stoningtonseafood.com) opened in Maine, doing both mail order and wholesale. Operating out of Portland, **Browne Trading Company** (www.brownetrading.com) transformed itself from a local fish wholesale and retail operation into a purveyor of fresh fish sourced both locally and internationally to the celebrity chef/white tablecloth restaurant market in New York. At the same time, they added an extensive line of smoked fish, including several smoked salmons with nontraditional curing ingredients, bearing the imprints of Daniel Boulud and Charlie Trotter. Some of their salmon products are available through Whole Foods Markets and through Fox & Obel in Chicago, with a wide assortment obtainable through mail order.

Joining Acme of Brooklyn in the New York City area, Perona Farms of New Jersey and Catskill Artisan Smokehouse provide smoked salmon to Fairway Markets and others in the area, with Perona distributing more widely through wholesale.

On the West Coast, two recent additions since the early 1990s include **Girard & Dominique Seafoods** (www.gourmetseafoods.com), based in Seattle and smoking Atlantic salmon as well as West Coast varieties of salmon and other fish such as sable.

Mail Order Sources: In addition to Ducktrap and Browne Trading Company, there are several other year-round or seasonal sources of smoked salmon and other fish—usually trout, mackerel, sable, sturgeon, haddock, scallops, and mussels. **Mackenzie Limited** (www.mackenzieltd.com) offers salmon from Scotland along with Ducktrap products; **Dean & Deluca** (www.deandeluca .com) carries products from Browne Trading Company; **Williams-Sonoma** (www.williams-sonoma.com) offers traditional English smoked salmon from H. Forman & Sons for the holidays. And of course there's **Petrossian** (www.petrossian.com), with the highest prices for just about everything.

Durham's Tracklements and Smokery of Ann Arbor sells smoked salmon by mail, online (www. tracklements.com), at its retail location (call ahead) at 212 E. Kingsley St. (734-930-6642), and by appointment. Durham's Classic

Highland smoked salmon is featured on the menu at Café Zola on West Washington Street off Main Street in Ann Arbor, and retail packages are available at Morgan & York on Packard Road south of Stadium Boulevard. **Zingerman's** Deli (www.zingermans.com), just up the street from the smokery, carries several exclusive specialty cured and smoked salmons from Tracklements, as well as trout, mackerel, and, in season, Alaskan sable. Tracklements' cold-smoked salmons are cured using only hand-rubbed dry cure, without brining. Seasoned cold-smoked salmons, which Tracklements introduced in the early 1990s (Gravlax, Pastrami, Thai-Spice, Santa Fe, Peppered), use freshly hand-ground spices and chopped fresh herbs for aromatic infusions. Favorites among the different smokes offered are Hardwood (a Tracklements Classic), Pecan wood, Alderwood, and Cherry. Twice-smoked salmon, drier and firmer than the others, has its loyal following as well. Tracklements' hot-smoked salmons are cured in lightly seasoned brines or marinades (Miso/Mirin, Tandoori, Chipotle/Adobo). The signature Single Malt Whisky cured and rubbed salmon is now done only for the poet Robert Burns's birthday in late January or by special order. Irish whiskey cured and peat-smoked salmon is available in time for St. Patrick's Day.

For Spanish products such as smoked paprika, vinegars, and oils, the **La Tienda** company is a good source. Order online at www.latienda.com. Another source for Spanish foods is www.spanishtable.com.

Blood-orange olive oil, as well as other uniquely flavored oils and vinegars, can be purchased from **Stonehouse Olive Oil** (www.stonehouseoliveoil.com).

Late-harvest moscatel vinegar, olive oils, cheeses, and an extensive selection of wines can be found at **Morgan & York** in Ann Arbor www.morganandyork.com

Caviar, coffee, cheese, deli items, and thousands of other products can be found at the famed New York City deli **Zabar's** (www.zabars.com).

Recipe Index

Pollack

Chunky "Skillet Hash de Brandade"
  with Smoked Fish, 108
Classic Smooth Brandade, 106
Kedgeree, 92
Seafood Chili with Smoked Fish, 74
Semismooth Brandade, 107

Sable

Seared Cold-Smoked Sable or
  Black Cod with Greens and
  Vinaigrette, 58
Smoked Sable "Carpaccio"
  with Citrus Salad and Da Vero
  Olive Oil, 62
Smoked-Sablefish and
  Potato Salad, 103

Salmon

Alycia's Smoked-Salmon
  Toasts with Cucumber and
  Greek Yogurt, 26
Arugula and Snow-Pea
  Salad with Smoked Salmon, 60
Asparagus Velouté with Smoked Salmon, 67
Avocado and Smoked-Salmon "Salsa"
  on Jícama Chips, 24
Belgian Endive "Canoes" with Hot-
  Smoked Salmon or Trout, 23
Blanched or Grilled Asparagus with
  Smoked Salmon, 24
Corn Chowder with Smoked Fish, 68
Crispy Polenta Rounds with
  Smoked Salmon, 28
Cucumber Slices with
  Smoked Salmon, Pickled
  Ginger, and Chive, 23
Do-Ahead Risotto with Smoked Fish
  or Shellfish, 91
Fettuccine Alfredo with
  Smoked Salmon, 81
Fettuccine with Smoked
  Salmon, Arugula, and Endive, 84

Grilled or Sautéed Cold-Smoked Salmon or
  Gravlax, with Arugula and Romaine, 56
Linguine with Smoked Salmon
  and Scallions, 78
Meredith's Pasta with Smoked
  Salmon and Olives, 79
Orecchiette and White Beans with
  Hot-Smoked Salmon or Cod, 87
Orzo with Wild Rice and Smoked
  Fish or Shellfish, 90
Pasta Primavera with Smoked
  Salmon or Trout, 82
Penne with Asparagus, Smoked Salmon,
  and Sesame Seeds, 83
Pita Bread with Greek Yogurt and
  Smoked Salmon, 38
Pizza with Chèvre and
  Smoked Salmon, 95
Risotto with Peas and
  Smoked Salmon, 88
Roasted Golden Beets with
  Smoked Fish, 54
Smoked Salmon and Salmon Roe
  on Crispy Potato Pancakes with
  Horseradish Cream and
  Pickled Onions, 49
Smoked-Salmon and Shrimp Ravioli, 86
Smoked-Salmon Bruschetta
  with Horseradish Cream, 20
Smoked-Salmon Bruschetta
  with Tomato and Avocado, 21
Smoked-Salmon Cakes with
  Red-Pepper Sauce, 43
Smoked-Salmon Chowder, 70
Smoked-Salmon Dumplings with
  Meyer Lemon Vinaigrette, 45
Smoked Salmon on Rye Toasts
  with Cucumber and Red Onion, 22
Smoked-Salmon "Pinwheel" Wraps
  with Lavash and Mascarpone, 34
Smoked-Salmon Tartare I, 32
Smoked-Salmon Tartare II, 33
Smoked-Salmon Toasts with Egg
  Salad and Arugula, 27

Smoked-Salmon Tortillas, 37
Southwestern Black Bean and
  Corn Salad with Smoked
  Salmon or Cod, 104
Thai Fish Cakes, 40
Tomato, Chickpea, and
  Smoked-Salmon Salad, 52
Tortellini Salad with
  Smoked Salmon, 55
Tortellini with Smoked
  Salmon and Dill, 85
Tricia's Inspiration, 25
Vietnamese Spring Rolls, 39
White Bean Salad with Smoked
  Salmon, 53

Scallops

Mediterranean Chowder with
  Smoked Haddock and Scallops, 65
Orzo with Wild Rice and Smoked
  Fish or Shellfish, 90
Seared Smoked Sea Scallops with
  Greens and Vinaigrette, 57

Trout

Belgian Endive "Canoes" with
  Hot-Smoked Salmon or Trout, 23
Chunky Smoked-Trout Spread, 35
Do-Ahead Risotto with Smoked
  Fish or Shellfish, 91
Kuku with Smoked Trout, 101
Pasta Primavera with Smoked
  Salmon or Trout, 82
Salade Niçoise with Smoked
  Mackerel, Bluefish, or Trout, 59
Smoked-Trout, Cucumber, and
  Radish Salad with Cilantro Cream, 61
Smoked-Trout and Potato Salad
  with Chives, 102

Whitefish

Peterson's Temptation, 97

Index